# OVEN TEMPERATURES

| GAS | ½ | 1 | 2 | 3 | 4 | 5 | 6 | 7 | 8 | 9 |
|---|---|---|---|---|---|---|---|---|---|---|
| FAHRENHEIT | 275° | 300° | 325° | 350° | 375° | 400° | 425° | 450° | 475° | 500° |
| CENTIGRADE | 135° | 149° | 163° | 177° | 190° | 205° | 218° | 232° | 246° | 260° |

# WEIGHTS

| BRITISH | ½ oz | 1 oz | 2 oz | 3 oz | 4 oz | 8 oz ½ lb | 16 oz 1 lb | 32 oz 2 lb |
|---|---|---|---|---|---|---|---|---|
| METRIC (approx) | 15g | 30g | 60g | 90g | 120g | 240g | 480g | Not quite 1 kilo |
| AMERICAN | | ¼ stick | ½ stick | | 1 stick | 2 sticks | 4 sticks | 8 sticks |

# MEASURES

| Imperial Pints & Fluid ounces | 1 fl oz | 2 fl oz | 3 fl oz | 4 fl oz | 5 fl oz | 6 fl oz | 7 fl oz | 8 fl oz | 9 fl oz | ½ pt. 10 fl oz |
|---|---|---|---|---|---|---|---|---|---|---|
| Metric (approx) | 30ml | 60ml | 90ml | 120ml | 145ml | 170ml | 200ml | 230ml | 260ml | 280ml |
| AMERICAN | | ¼ cup | | ½ cup | | | | 1 cup | | |

The Imperial ½ pt = 10 fl oz     1 pt = 20 fl oz.
The USA ½ pt = 8 fl oz     1 pt = 16 fl oz.
35 fl oz = almost a litre or 1000 mls.

The American measuring tablespoon is smaller than the
British so use an American tablespoon plus a teaspoon = 1 Br. tablespoon.
American measuring teaspoons are also smaller than British.
4 British tablespoons = 2½ fl oz.

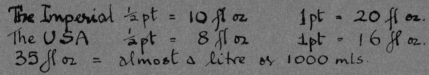

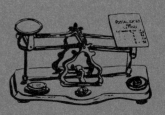

# RECIPES

## TO

# RELISH

## GOOD COOKING & ENTERTAINING

# AT HOME

by

Joan Wolfenden

For John and Rosalind
without whom
none of this could have
happened nor
Peacock Vane
continued.

First published in Great Britain by Peacock Vane,
Bonchurch, Isle of Wight 1979.
Reprinted by Pelham Books Ltd. 44 Bedford Square,
London W.C.1. 1981.

ISBN 0 7207 1303 X

Printed in Singapore

# CONTENTS

# CHAPTER ONE.

## The Stock Pot ~ Soups ~ Herbs & Simples

Double, double toil and trouble;
Fire burn and cauldron bubble ~

So many misconceptions about stock pots!
They are not necessarily stirred by three witches
on a blasted heath! All you have to do with
the stock pot is to keep it in a cool place & bring
it to the boil for two or three minutes every twenty
four hours ~ Excess fat can be removed when it
is cold. Much appreciated on the bird table

DONT USE VEGETABLE water. This is splendid
for adding to soups, gravies and sauces but if it's
put into the pot it usually sours it. Raw bones
are better than cooked ones; but both may go in.
Cover them with cold water ~ add a roughly
chopped onion ~ a little skin colours the stock
pleasantly ~ a bouquet garni and perhaps
some celery leaves. I rather delight in
salvaging this despised foliage from people's
cheese plates! A homely carrot is useful.
Bring very slowly to the boil and simmer
gently for a long time. The modern
simmering gas is excellent ~

# HERBS & SIMPLES ~

## THE BOUQUET GARNI

Usually a little bunch of <u>Parsley</u> and its stems, <u>Thyme</u> & <u>Bay leaf</u>.

**Pork** and **Duck** go with <u>Sage</u>, <u>apples</u> and <u>oranges</u>

**Beef** calls for Horseradish <u>Costmary</u>* and Mustard

\* Also called Alecost.

# HOW TO CHOP AN ONION

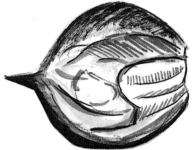

Peel the onion down
towards the root.
Cut away the root.

Cut the onion in half
lengthways and quickly
place both halves face
down on the chopping board.

Cut the half into five or
six lengthways.

Now cut across at
right angles and you
have a chopped onion
and no crying.

# SOUPS.

My best soups "occur" when the stock is separated from it's old bones and each day fresh ones are added — chop bones, bacon rinds, giblets, lamb knuckles from the shoulder. Eventually the stock is so rich that a glass of sherry and a little salt make a good thin soup.       If you prefer a

Clear Soup or Consommé use a whipped egg white. Stir this into the cold stock and bring slowly to the boil stirring often. Let it cool a little and strain through a hair sieve or a nylon stocking. A bright stock should result.

Julienne is this type of stock in which shreds of raw vegetables are cooked — carrot, celery, petit pois etc.

Brodo is the Italian clear soup made from chicken stock and in which vermicelli or spaghetti is poached. This is the origin of the commercial chicken noodle soup.

Peasant Soup which covers the "everything but the kitchen sink" variety is my favourite. Part of its charm is its different taste each time it is made!       Chop and fry an onion in butter — or the fat saved from the stock pot. Lid on, low heat, twenty minutes. Now add stock, a chopped pimento, a chicken liver, tomatoes, root vegetables cut in dice — a handful of grated cheese and some chopped fresh herbs. Add salt and pepper to taste. A little wine, sherry or vermouth. The possibilities are endless. Remember it is impossible to cook without tasting and adjusting the flavours.

# LOBSTER SOUP
4 generous helpings.

2 lobster shells made into stock by summering them in chicken stock. 1 onion chopped + cooked in butter or olive oil until transparent (lid on, low heat, 20 minutes)

1 tablespoon mayonnaise or salad cream.

1 handful grated cheese. Juice of ½ a lemon.

Summer the onion, mayonnaise, cheese & lemon juice together, stirring for a minute or two. Add a cup of creamy milk or single cream and any little pieces of lobster meat salvaged from the thin claws & the carcase.

1 pt of lobster stock and a drip of cochineal to improve the colour. Putting the onion skin in the original stock before summering helps a lot. Without cosmetics the soup tends to look grey and unpleasant.

1 dessertspoon of turmeric is now added which improves both the flavour and the appearance. The soup is further improved by a cupful of fresh chopped lobster meat or prawns. Serve garnished with a thin slice of lemon. It needs very little salt and pepper. If a thicker soup is preferred put a tablespoon of thick commercial chicken soup in a little white wine & add.

# PEASANT BROTH (robuster than Peasant soup)
1 onion chopped + fried (lid on, low heat, 20 mins.)
2 pints good stock. A pimento cut small.
1 tablespoon oats, 1 tablespoon pearl barley,
1 tablespoon lentils. Salt & pepper.

Cook very slowly and add seasoning and chopped parsley to taste. (Contd on p. 10)

Peasant broth ( Contd. from p.8 ) This is a magic gruel and good for a hungry family. It can be put in a casserole and "forgotten" in a low oven. If it becomes too thick, thin with a little vegetable water (pea or carrot is best — or even some more stock.)

Mint chops well on a chopping board with a sharp knife. Sprinkle generously with granulated sugar and it chops readily.

When mint is growing strongly in the garden it is a good idea to chop masses and freeze into little cubes in the ice trays. These can be stored in a polythene bag in the deep freeze. One cube, in the depths of winter makes two or three servings of mint sauce.

Chives are quickly chopped by holding in a bundle and cutting through the lot with a pair of scissors.

Nasturtium flowers, borage flowers, marigold petals and the flowers of chives all mixed in a green or rice salad add a very pleasing touch of colour — all taste of the herbs and are very edible.

Seasoned flour. I like to keep this in a honey jar in the fridge. About 4oz of plain flour. I teaspoon of sea salt, a generous amount of freshly milled black pepper. I teaspoon of chopped parsley, I teaspoon chopped thyme. Use it for tossing stewing meat or chicken before frying & for use in casseroles et cetera ~ ~

Lamb needs:
Mint   Rosemary.   Cucumber,   Onion

and red currant jelly.

Fish; Fennel, Onion, Cucumber,
Lemon Rind

and Mushrooms      Cheese

garlic and   tomato.

Chicken loves

<u>tarragon</u> <u>Marjoram,</u> Watercress

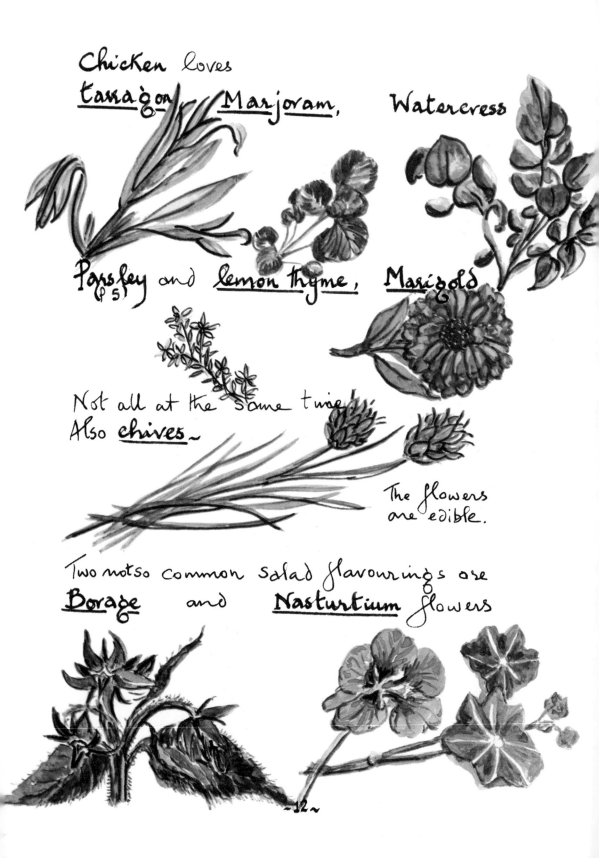

<u>Parsley</u> and <u>lemon thyme</u>, <u>Marigold</u>
(p 5)

Not all at the same time!
Also <u>chives</u>~

The flowers
are edible.

Two not so common Salad flavourings are
<u>Borage</u> and <u>Nasturtium</u> flowers

## Ttoro

This is a substantial dish and will make a good supper if followed by fresh fruit and cheese. It should be served with hot crisp french bread. (Recipe on page 151)

1 medium sized onion chopped fine & cooked transparent in olive oil (lid on. low heat 20 mins.)

1 clove of garlic crushed.

1 teaspoon turmeric

1 tablespoon tomato Ketchup.

      Fry these together until bubbling nicely

1 pinch of sugar

1 teaspoonful of chopped sorrel leaves

1 Medium tin of Italian peeled tomatoes

    Add these ingredients being careful to Keep the tomatoes whole.

For 4 portions you need

4 x 2 oz fingers of raw white fish. (Haddock is very suitable)

4 oz raw scampi.

    Simmer the fish and Scampi in a very little chicken stock for 30 seconds.

Serve the fish equally into 4 soup plates & add one tomato to each. Keep hot in the oven.

Now add the chicken/fish stock to the Soup & boil rapidly for 5 minutes and reduce a little in volume. Test for seasoning adding salt and pepper to taste. Pour over the four prepared portions & send to table with a large dollop of garlic flavoured mayonnaise in each dish!

French Sorrel

Wild Sorrel.

~13~

## POTAGE JEANNETTE

This is a by-product of home made cream cheese (p 149). Cut 2 small or 1 large onion into thin rings and simmer until tender in a cupful of chicken stock. Add 1½ pts whey. Thicken with commercial white onion soup smoothed in a cup of creamy milk or make a roux with 1 oz of butter and 1 oz flour adding the milk to this. Now toss in a handful of grated cheese. Taste and season with salt and black pepper. Serve with a large dollop of whipped cream or natural yoghourt well seasoned with chopped chives.

## POTAGE ANDALOUSE

Another type of the "peasant" soup. Cook a coffee cup of rice in stock (preferably chicken). Add peeled tomatoes and chopped onions. When tender whip with an egg whisk and add a tablespoon of chopped marjoram or oregano. Taste and flavour with salt and pepper. Grated cheese, also, may be added.

## MARROW SOUP

This is a by-product of the marrow cooked in butter, onion and tomato on page 72. Take any marrow left and it's juice and whisk well. Fry a chopped onion in butter until transparent, add a finely chopped pimiento, a handful of grated cheese and the marrow juices. Simmer for 10 minutes and serve with croutons.

CROUTONS Little cubes of stale brown and/or white bread fried crisp in dripping, butter or oil

# Rings of onion. for Jeannette~

Parsley chops best in a tea cup and using a sharp pair of scissors. As you cut the pieces fall back upon the scissors to be cut & re-cut. Don't remove the stems. They have the most flavour ~~

## CHICKEN & PARSLEY SOUP

This is a by-product of boiled chicken (page 37). To any left over parsley sauce add some of the chicken stock, the juice of half a lemon, a tablespoon of quick oats and 2 tablespoons cream. Add salt and freshly ground black pepper. Alternatively leave out the oats and serve with croutons and some more chopped parsley.

# WATERCRESS SOUP     6 helpings.

A bunch of watercress
1 onion, 1 large potato.
1 pt milk, 1 pt water.
Salt, pepper and a little cream or yoghourt.

Reserve the very best leaves of the watercress.
Roughly chop the onion, the potato and the rest of
the watercress and the stems.  Simmer in the
cold water until tender ~ about 20 minutes.
Pass through a mouli or liquidize.

Return to the saucepan.  Add the milk
and bring to the boil.  Taste and season.

Serve with a little cream or yoghourt
to which the best leaves (chopped) have been added.


# AVGOLEMONO   (Greek Egg & Lemon Soup)

2 eggs,   2 lemons,   1 teacup of cooked rice.
2 pints white stock (chicken or veal is best)
Salt & pepper.

Simmer the cooked rice in the stock until
overcooked.  Add the lemon juice hot.

Beat the eggs in a warm soup tureen ~
first the whites, then add the yolks.  Now
add the soup a cupful at a time and beat into
the fluffy eggs.  Serve at once.

This is an interesting different taste
and very suitable in summer before a cold
lunch with salad.     Sufficient for 6 helpings.

## CHESTNUT & TURKEY SOUP

This is one of the good dishes that can be made with the minimum effort after Christmas.

You need ~ A cup of chestnut stuffing
A cup of finely shredded turkey and/or the muddle in the inside of the carcass.
2 mushrooms chopped fine.
1 tablespoon chopped parsley.
1 cup whipped cream.
1½ pts of turkey stock.

Simmer the chestnuts & turkey meat in the stock. Taste & add salt & pepper if necessary.

Serve into soup plates. Then add a tablespoon to each plate of the cream mixed with the raw mushrooms & parsley. A glass of sherry added just before the cream is added lifts this soup onto a higher plane!

# POTAGE MANDARIN

For 4:
1 Cup of orange sauce left over from caneton
       à l'orange.
1 Cup duck stock.
1 medium sized tin of Italian tomatoes (sieved)
1 oz butter, or duck fat.
1 onion chopped, sage.
1 coffee spoon curry powder
Salt, black pepper, sugar.

This is a splendid by-product of Caneton à l'orange (p.122). With the cup of sauce, the stock and tomato at the ready make the soup by:

Frying the onion in the fat (low heat, lid on, 20 minutes). Stir in the curry powder.

Add a little chopped sage and all the fluid.

Taste and season with salt, freshly milled black pepper and sugar. If you like a thicker soup add a little commercial tomato soup mix. I prefer the thinner soup garnished with croutons.

## COEURs des LAITUEs (lettuce hearts)

This should be made of lettuce hearts but I gather up the young leaves and stems of "bolting" lettuces and use these. Serve either as a vegetable ~ or liquidise with milk and serve as soup

Chop an onion and summer in butter. Add lettuce moist from washing, salt and pepper and summer with the lid on until tender.

When served as a vegetable the natural juices can be thickened with beurre manié. (p.35)

# ARTICHOKE SOUP

For 6 servings:
2 lbs Jerusalem artichokes
1 pt water, 1 oz butter,
½ oz flour, 1 pt milk.
Salt & freshly ground pepper.
1 large onion (chopped & cooked in
butter for 20 minutes)
2 oz grated cheese.

Scrub the artichokes. Cook in the water until tender. Rub through a mouli legume or liquidize. If the artichokes are chopped roughly they cook in about 15 minutes. Add the pulp and the cooking water to the onion. Add the milk in which the flour has been mixed. Bring to the boil; add the cheese and having tasted add salt and freshly ground black pepper to please the palate. A little double cream added at the last minute provides a luxurious soup.

They look much more appetizing after scrubbing!

# Spinach & Egg Soup.

For 6 servings.

2lbs spinach cooked, just covered in water for two or three minutes. Sieve, reserving the liquid or liquidize. Add 1pt of milk in which is smoothed a little commercial Asparagus soup. Now taste and add salt and freshly ground black pepper. Simmer for two or three minutes. Warm a soup tureen. Separate the whites from the yolks of two eggs. Whip the whites stiff in the warm tureen. Now whip in the yolks and gradually add the soup to the eggs stirring constantly.

Serve at once or the eggs will spoil.

It is possible to make this soup well in advance and re-heat. Only the ceremony of the eggs must be left to the last minute.

# TOMATO SOUP

For 4 helpings:     1½ lbs tomatoes
                    2 oz butter, 1 level teaspoon curry paste.
                    A pinch of basil, or 6 leaves chopped.
                    ½ pt chicken stock.
                    Salt, pepper, sugar.
                    2 tablespoons double cream.

Melt the butter and fry the curry paste for a minute or so. Peel the tomatoes. Pour boiling water over them. Empty it away quickly and replace with cold. They then peel without any waste. Cut them in half and remove the fibrous bit where the stem joins the fruit.

Simmer in the butter mixture with the lid on for twenty minutes. Beat with an egg whisk. Add ½ pint chicken stock and the basil. Taste and add salt, pepper and about a teaspoon of demerara. It depends on the ripeness of the fruit how much sugar is needed. Stir in the cream and serve. If a smoother soup is preferred it can be liquidized or pressed through a mouli.

# MUSHROOM SOUP. (Rosalind's recipe).

For 6 good helpings.
12 medium sized mushrooms.
1 onion.   2 oz butter.   1 oz flour.
¼ pt red wine   ¾ pt stock.
¾ pt milk   ¼ pt cream.
Salt and pepper.

Mince the mushroomstems and the onion (or chop roughly) and simmer in the stock and wine for about 20 minutes. Lid off as it needs to reduce a little. Pass through a mouli.

Melt the butter and fry in the flour and use the milk to make a sauce. Slice the mushroom caps thinly and add them and the mushroom stem stock. Bring to the boil. Taste. Add salt and pepper and pour in the cream. Heat again but do not boil the cream.

The less the caps are cooked the better the flavour of the soup will be.

# POTAGE PRINCESSE

In 1½ pts of strong chicken stock cook one chopped onion, 6 chopped sticks of asparagus and a cup of peas. When tender liquidize, taste and add salt and pepper. Garnish with whipped cream mixed with chopped parsley & chives.

# CHAPTER TWO

## General observations on Cooking. Sauces, Casseroles, Pies & Winning Ways with leftovers.

General observations on Stock & Soups were expressed in Chapter One.

My bible on cooking is the old Mrs Beeton printed at the turn of the century. So often she is criticized for saying: "Take a dozen eggs", but she does not say it very often and she _is_ the authority on British cooking.

In the days of the British Raj the meat grown in Britain on our lush pastures encouraged by our liberal rainfall was second to none. So good that all that was necessary was boiling water and salt to make a wonderful dish. Boiled Beef & Carrots for instance. Or a large piece of prime beef was roasted on a spit in front of a clear fire! What could be more splendid?

When the first & second world wars hit us and the family servant(s) disappeared we all discovered that the "good plain cook" and the British condemnation of discussing food at table as "bad manners" were both not only "dead ducks" but non-existent.

This in my opinion was the birth of Good British Cooking. Our recipes are a polyglot collection and good food is the order of the day.

This book is about cooking. Not many recipes are given as there are too many good cookery books available full of first class information. The recipes given are meant to be a little different and not so well known. The general observations apply to all recipes. The cunning use of herbs and spices puts magic into the pot and that is what this book is seeking to achieve. One of the easiest mistakes for a keen cook to make is, having achieved a really excellent sauce, and having succeeded, proceeds to use the same formula until everything cooked tastes alike.

Magic in cooking comes when everything tastes different and the palate is surprised into a state of happiness.

Now that our food and restaurants are both extra expensive there is a great satisfaction in having a festive meal at home as a treat. The money saved on eating out can be invested in little extravagances and is there anything more pleasant than a happy table of diners enjoying eachother, old fashioned conversation and memorable food?

Chapter IX concentrates on dishes suitable for home entertaining.

# SAUCES

## ONION SAUCE

This is one of our best British sauces. ~ So simple that it defies the Continental chef. I have yet to meet one who can make it!

Cut 2 onions up roughly and simmer for 10 minutes in cold water which barely covers the onion. Mix 1 oz plain flour with a cup of creamy milk and stir into the hot onion and water mixture. Add 2 ozs of butter and salt and freshly ground black pepper to taste. It is just as easy as that! It is a good thing to make this sauce in larger quantities as it is the perfect base for one of the peasant soups mentioned earlier.

## SAUCE FOR SHELLFISH COCKTAILS.

2 tablespoons double cream
2 tablespoons mayonnaise (p. 26)
2 tablespoons tomato Ketchup.
1 tablespoon brandy or dry sherry.
Mix well together.
This should be enough
for 4 generous helpings.

## CUCUMBER SAUCE    (A hot sauce).

This is a useful sauce for lamb in the winter or for hot salmon at any time of the year.

FOR 6 PORTIONS:    2 oz butter,

½ cucumber diced (peeled or not; it is just a matter of individual taste).

1 large chopped onion (cooked in the butter on low heat).

1 Cup double cream or 1 cup milk mixed with 1 oz flour.

Salt, pepper added to taste.

Add the cucumber to the hot transparent onion. Let it simmer slowly for another 20 minutes with the lid on at very low heat. Add the cream or milk and flour. Bring to the boil and remove from the heat. Add salt and freshly milled pepper.

There used to be a pub somewhere in the North called: "The Lamb & Cucumber". I couldn't find a recipe anywhere so contrived this one. Apparently the dish was popular in the reign of Elizabeth I. Borage stems used to be used for their cucumber flavour. Presumably they could be used instead of the cucumber.

## MAYONNAISE

There are many modern recipes for mayonnaise using electric whisks and liquidizers.

The old fashioned wooden spoon and pudding basin variety, when making a small quantity, is second to none.

2 egg yolks. (use the whites for meringues or for garnishing soup.)

1 level teaspoon dry mustard.

1 level teaspoon salt. Black pepper.

6 oz olive oil.

Enough good malt vinegar, wine vinegar or lemon juice to sharpen the blandness.

Thoroughly mix the egg yolks, mustard, salt and pepper in a dry pudding basin using a wooden spoon and always turning the same way — whichever is the most comfortable. Relax, sit down and feel at peace. Now gradually add the oil being careful not to curdle the mayonnaise by too much enthusiasm. As the mixture emulsifies it is possible to be more reckless with the oil. When all is mixed add the vinegar or other acid to taste.

Should the mayonnaise curdle start again with a fresh egg yolk, mustard & pepper, and gradually add the curdled mixture. The third egg means that a little more oil will be needed.

## TARTARE SAUCE

Half fill the bowl or sauce boat you are going to use at table with mayonnaise.

Add 1 tablespoon of chopped chives & parsley. 1 chopped firm tomato, 1 chopped pimento 1 stick chopped celery, 4 chopped gherkins and a spoonful of capers.

Stir gently and it is ready

## CUCUMBER SAUCE (Cold ~ for use with cold fish).

1 cup double cream whipped stiff ~ but not to butter.
Salt & freshly ground black pepper.
Add a tablespoon of good quality malt vinegar,
wine vinegar, apple cider vinegar or lemon juice.
Stir the acid in a few drops at a time as though
making mayonnaise.

Cut ¼ cucumber into dice. Skinned or not is a
matter of taste. Old wives tales say that the skin
contains a digestive. I like the feel and colour of
the skin.

Dry the diced cucumber in a clean cloth and stir
gently into the cream mixture. If preferred
half the cream may be replaced by mayonnaise.

## SAUCE ROBERT.

This is a classic French sauce. I believe
they serve it with steak. I think it goes very
well with roasted pork and sage and onion
stuffing instead of apple sauce. In fact I have
been told by one of our customers that it is the
best apple sauce he had ever tasted!

For 4 good helpings you need:
1 large or 2 medium onions chopped and
sweated in 1oz butter. (lid on, low heat. 20 mins).
Now barely cover the transparent onion with
equal quantities of good malt vinegar and
white wine. Simmer with the lid on for 20
minutes. This requires very low heat ~

even the use of an asbestos mat.

In the sauce boat in which it is to be served put 1 level teaspoon of dry mustard, 1 level teaspoon of granulated sugar, and 1 teaspoon of vinegar and mix well together.

Pour the hot onion/vinegar/wine mixture on to this. Stir well; add salt and pepper to taste and serve.

This sauce keeps well in a closed jar in a refrigerator if you are in the mood to make a larger quantity. It is also a splendid starter for a peasant soup.


## BOLSHEVIK SAUCE (just plain Red).

One day I wanted a new sauce to serve with escalop de veau Cordon Bleu; took all my library of cookery books to bed and delved. Nothing quite answered. The search was for something piquant~ of a good colour and not too highly flavoured. A hot bath inspired:

Cook a chopped onion in butter (lid on, low heat, 20 minutes). Add a small sieved tin of Italian peeled tomatoes and a small tin of red pimentoes chopped and their juice. Now add a teaspoon of lemon juice & a teaspoon of worcester sauce. Add a little sugar. Basil brings out the tomato taste. Add salt & black pepper. If necessary simmer to reduce and thicken the sauce.

# MUSHROOM SAUCE (Rosalind's Recipe).

1 oz butter.

2 oz fresh button mushrooms cut in slices (stems & all).

A quarter of a lemon squeezed.

Enough double cream to float the mushrooms.

Cook the sliced mushrooms in the butter briefly. Squeeze on the lemon juice. Add the cream and just make it hot. Do not boil.

Add salt & freshly ground pepper to taste.

# BREAD SAUCE

This is a very easy way of making this excellent British sauce. Peel on onion and stick it with four cloves. Simmer in ½ pt of milk and ½ pt of water with the lid on. After 20 minutes the onion should be tender. Liquidize fresh white breadcrumbs and add them to the milk, onion and water mixture until it is as thick as double cream. Season with salt and pepper and stir in a good knob of butter. Use the sauce straight away or it becomes stodgy. Cream may be added.

# PARSLEY SAUCE

1 oz butter, 1 oz plain flour, ¼ pt creamy milk. ¼ pt strong chicken stock. 2 tablespoons chopped parsley, salt and pepper.

Make a roux by melting the butter, stirring in the flour and adding the fluids to make a good smooth sauce. Add the parsley, salt & pepper. If the sauce is for fish use fish velouté instead of chicken stock.

# PRAWN SAUCE

½ lb shelled prawns
1 coffee cup of cream
1 coffee cup real mayonnaise
1 coffee cup tomato ketchup
Mix well. Add a dash of brandy if you wish.

For the Devonshire Hake recipe (p 93) both
these sauces should be doubled in quantity

# MINT SAUCE

Our family recipe for mint sauce is a
small jug nearly full of the chopped, sugary
mint. (p. 10).        Add equal quantities of
water and mature malt vinegar. Barely
cover the mint and stir well adding more
sugar to taste. If using young fresh mint from
the garden don't discard the stems. If they
are tender they are full of flavour.

# BEURRE BLANC  sufficient for 4.

4 shallots or 1 small onion very finely chopped.
1 glass white wine. 1 tablespoon wine or malt vinegar.
4 oz butter cut into small cubes (like loaf sugar)
Boil down the shallots, wine and vinegar to a mush.
Remove pan from heat and beat in two of the butter
cubes with a wire whisk. Return to minimal heat and
beat in the rest one at a time whisking constantly.

This will keep hot on a hot plate but not in a
double saucepan. Really it should be served
immediately it is ready. Excellent with fish.

Left over sauce is good melted on green vegetables.

~31~

## SCAMPI and PRAWN SAUCE

This is a good sauce to serve with grilled white fish.
It also makes a good filling for savoury pancakes.
¼ lb scampi.   2oz peeled prawns.
2oz butter    1 coffee cup sherry.   1 coffee cup cream.
1 egg yolk.  Salt, pepper, cayenne, mace, lemon peel
grated fine.  1 teaspoon plain flour.

Chop the scampi and fry in the butter. Sprinkle
in the flour.  Pour in the sherry and the cream and
only just bring to the boil.  Mix the yolk with a little
cream and stir into the hot sauce.  Taste and season
with salt, pepper, cayenne, mace and the lemon zest.
Add the prawns.  Nearly bring to the boil and serve
at once.  If you get it too hot the egg will curdle. If
faint hearted you
can use a double
sauce pan.  I'm too
impatient.

## APPLE SAUCE

4 bramley apples peeled and sliced.   1oz butter.
1 tablespoon water.  Cook slowly with the lid on.
The sauce is ready when it goes into a natural
purée – usually about 15-20 minutes.
If this sauce is left over it can be sweetened
and used for other apple pudding dishes.

# CHEESE SAUCE

I am so fond of cheese sauce and use it such a lot that I fear I may qualify for the criticism at the middle of page 24! However it is very easy to make. For a pint you will need:

1½ oz butter, 1½ oz flour, 4 oz grated cheese.
1 pint fluid made up of milk, stock, wine, beer or cider. Salt and pepper. For a stronger flavour use a little mustard as well.

Make a roux with the flour and butter ~ just getting the butter melted before stirring them together. Gradually add the liquid and finally the cheese and seasoning. If you are impatient and achieve a few lumps either liquidize or rub through a sieve. This makes more washing up and it is easier and quicker to do it a bit slower in the first place ~~

# EGG SAUCE.

This is made the same way as the cheese sauce using a pint of milk and stock with white wine, cider or dry sherry and 1½ oz each of flour and butter. Hard boil 4 eggs. Slice 2 in rounds and chop the other two very small. Stir into the white sauce and add salt and pepper to taste.

# SAUCE BEARNAISE

2 fluid oz wine vinegar  3 shallots.
2 egg yolks.  4 oz butter.
Tarragon.  (fresh is better but dried will do).

Chop the shallots and simmer in the vinegar with a little bunch of tarragon.  Chop and reserve the best leaves for use later.  When there is just a moist mess on the bottom of the pan, add a little water and reduce again.  Rub through a sieve and add two egg yolks.  Put into a double saucepan and stir in lump by lump the 4 oz of soft butter.  Add salt, pepper and the rest of the tarragon.

If this sauce starts to curdle remove from the heat, put in a dessertspoonful of cold water and beat madly.

Another dodge (against all the rules) is to put in a dessertspoonful of beurre manié (p.35) before adding the egg yolks.  Cook for 30 seconds with the starter and then proceed as above.  I don't think that this spoils the sauce at all and it takes a lot of anxiety out of the performance.

## MINT BUTTER.  (John's recipe).

Make a sauce Béarnaise using garden mint instead of tarragon. Super with Rack of Lamb. (p.121).

# CHILLI SHERRY (Recipe from Kenya: Pili-pili hoho)

A ½ oz packet of dry chillies. Sherry.

Place the chillies in a bottle of sherry and leave to infuse for a fortnight. An empty Angostura bitters bottle is a good dispenser for this relish. It can be used in soups, stews, mince etc. Excellent in a clear soup~ but only a drop or two. It is made for the jaded colonial palate~~

## Beurre manié

This is the quick way to thicken almost anything. It is a good dodge to make quite a lot. Melt 4oz butter in a saucepan and stir in 4oz plain flour. Stir until smooth and doughlike. Store in a screw top jar in the fridge. Don't get the butter too hot ~ in summer it can be left to soften in a sunny place before mixing with the flour. A dessertspoonful may be added to boiling sauces, soups or stews if they need "instant" thickening.

## French dressing.

Olive oil, salt, mustard, sugar, black pepper. Wine Vinegar.

Mix 1 teaspoon each of salt, pepper and sugar with a little vinegar. Stir in a little dry mustard (I like a teaspoonful). Add the olive oil and a little vinegar. If kept in a glass stoppered bottle and shaken well before use it is always ready.

I use a cupful of oil with the above quantities Sometimes I break an egg into this relish.

# CASLEROLES, PIES and the like

## BELGIAN CASSEROLE (A family recipe).

Cut 1lb of stewing steak into 4 steaks.

In 2 oz of seasoned flour (p. 10) dry the 4
steaklets and fry on all sides in 2 oz butter.
Put the steak in a casserole. Now add 8 shallots_
whole but peeled, and toss in the buttery pan for a few
moments before adding to the steak. Next 4 carrots
cut in rings and 2 chicons of chicory cut into
four length ways. Dry them in the seasoned flour and
fry lightly in the buttery pan. Add more butter
if necessary. 4 dried prunes soaked overnight
in a small glass of red wine.

I slice wholemeal bread covered in French mustard.
Put any of the seasoned flour left over into the buttery
pan_ if necessary adding a little more butter. Make
a roux and add the red wine. Pour the resulting
sauce over the casserole. Add a bouquet garni made
of parsley, thyme and marjoram. Top with the
bread_ mustard side down.

Simmer for 2 to 2½ hours depending on
the toughness of the meat. If too thick add a little
stock (stir in the brown bread). If too thin add a
little beurre manié (p 35). Mother used to serve
this dish with baked jacket potatoes and a
tossed green salad.

## BOILED CHICKEN with parsley sauce

One of the best old-fashioned flavours is boiled chicken. These used to be cheap but seem no longer to exist. Perhaps they all end up in chicken flavoured cat and dog food. "Plastic" chickens are very good cooked this way

Cut an onion roughly and put it into a saucepan with a carrot, a stick of celery, 4 pepper corns, a teaspoon of salt and all the giblets except the liver. Put the chicken on top of this pot and enough boiling water to half cover the bird. When it reboils cover closely and reduce the heat to the minimum possible for about 45 minutes. Take out the chicken and when cool enough to handle carve into portions ~ ie. legs and thighs off and separated and the breast taken off in two good pieces. Take off all the little odds and ends and arrange in a casserole. Cover with parsley sauce (p 30) and simmer with the lid on for another half hour. Use half stock and half milk to make the sauce. The rest of the stock should make a beautiful soup. (p-15).

## SAUCE FOR SHOULDER of MUTTON (Elizabethan)

Take a spoonful of herbs (mint, rosemary) and as many capers. Half a pint of white wine, half a nutmeg and two eggs. Put a piece of butter to the gravy when it is boiled.

I presume the beaten eggs are added in a double saucepan ~

# GOULASH of VEAL

For 4 portions:    1 lb Veal (Butchers sometimes sell
                   oddments at more realistic prices)
    salt. pepper, paprika. onion,
    ¼ lb bacon, 3 potatoes, 1 pimento.

Remove all skin and fat from the veal and cut into dice.
Season well with salt, pepper & paprika. Fry a small
onion cut fine in butter until tender but not brown.
Now add the veal and fry turning gently every now and
again for 15 minutes.   The chopped pimento goes in now.
    While this is going on fry the bacon cut into dice
in butter and when it is half cooked add the potato -
peeled and diced - and fry together with the bacon
until golden.
    Now return to the first pan: sprinkle in a little
flour (as if making gravy) add a small cup of brown
stock and a similar quantity of Madeira or brown sherry.
Cover and simmer gently for another 15 minutes.
    Drain the potatoes & bacon (keep the fat for something
else - it is particularly good for fried bread or croutons)
Uncover the other brew and add the potatoes and bacon.
Stir well and continue cooking slowly - lid off - until
both the meat and potatoes are tender. Sprinkle with
chopped parsley and serve.

## KROMESKIS    (A White Russian Recipe)

2 chicken livers. 4 rashers streaky. A few mushrooms.
Make a panada by frying 1 oz butter & 1 oz flour together
until it leaves the side of the pan. Chop the livers and
mushrooms and mix with the panada. When cold wrap little
pieces in ½ rashers of bacon.   Dip in batter and fry

# RABBIT PIE (My Mother-in-law's recipe).

This recipe is only suitable for a wild rabbit.
Myxomatosis has put us all off rabbit. However,
occasionally a good one is available.

Cut into joints ~ do not chop as it splinters
the bones. Treat as if it is poultry ~ take off
the "wings" and the legs and break the backbone
into two. Simmer in poultry stock until
the meat will come away from the bones. When
cold enough to handle separate the meat from
the bones. Return the bones to the stock and
reduce until a rich stock arrives.

Grill ½lb of streaky bacon until nearly cooked.
Slice 4 onions and fry brown in the bacon fat.
Now layer in a pie dish rabbit, bacon, sprinkle
with sage and top with onion. Fill the pie with
layers. Thicken the stock and three-quarters
cover the contents of the pie. Cover with short
crust pastry (p 130) Bake for 35 minutes at
No 7 and the rest of the hour at No 2.

Bouquet
Garni

This one is of thyme, marjoram parsley & bayleaf.

## JUGGED HARE

1 hare - the meat cut away from the bone in
small pieces.    Make stock with the bones.
2 pts stock.
1 glass port. The juice of a lemon. 4oz butter.
1 oz seasoned flour (p 10) 2 shallots.
1 onion stuck with 4 cloves.   12 peppercorns.
Bouquet garni.     2 oz flour.

Toss the hare in seasoned flour and fry
in 2oz butter.  Place in a casserole with
the onion & cloves, the shallots chopped,
the pepper corns and the bouquet garni.
Pour on the port and cover with stock.
Cook slowly until tender.  About 2 hours
at No. 3.     Mix the other 2 oz of flour
with the rest of the butter & the lemon
juice, stir in to the gravy.  If you
have the blood this can be incorporated
at this stage  Fried veal stuffing balls are good with this.
(p 101).
Serve with red currant jelly.

## HARE SOUP

Any gravy and stock - or even hare
left mixed together with a spoonful
of red currant jelly make an excellent
soup.   To thicken either make a roux with
equal quantities of flour and butter and pour
in the soup or use a commercial kidney soup
mix and add a glass of red wine and a
generous teaspoonful of red currant jelly.

# CASSEROLE OF VEAL

2 lbs stewing veal cut into neat pieces.
4 oz butter.
3 carrots cut in rings. 3 celery sticks cut small.
1 onion cut into rings.  1 clove of garlic crushed.
1 glass white wine or cider.
1 small tin tomato puree & 1 teaspoon of sugar.
A bouquet garni.
1 tablespoon chopped parsley. 1 teaspoon grated lemon
                                                    rind.
Salt & pepper.  1 oz of flour.
Stock.

With half the butter fry the veal to brown and
seal the meat.   After about 5 minutes put the
meat into a casserole.   Melt the rest of the butter
and fry all the vegetables turning frequently until
they are golden brown.  Add the vegetables to the
casserole  and mix them with the meat.

Fry the flour in the buttery pan and stir in the wine,
tomato puree and the sugar.  Add the bouquet garni,
& season with salt and pepper.  Add enough stock so
that the gravy barely covers the meat.  Cover and
cook in a very slow oven for 1 or 2 hrs When the
meat and vegetables are tender remove from the
heat or the meat will become flabby and stringy.

Half fill a serving dish with freshly boiled
rice & spoon the meat & vegetables over. Finally
taste the gravy, adjust the seasoning and if
necessary thicken with beurre manié & pour
over.   This dish goes well with garden peas
cooked the French way with onion, lettuce and
baby carrots (p. 58 ).

# BEEFBURGERS   An American recipe.
### Ma Fronkie ~~

¾ lb fatty raw minced beef.
Tomato Ketchup.
1 egg.  Salt & pepper.
Quick oatmeal.

Break the egg into the centre of the mince.
Sprinkle with salt, pepper & tomato Ketchup.
Sprinkle with the quick oats.  Mix well and form
into 8 beefburgers.

They are best grilled & served with a piquant
or barbecue sauce.

## CHEESE & VEGETABLE PIE

This is useful for vegetarians! Apart from
this it makes a pleasant change.

2 lbs root crops ~ a mixture of potatoes, carrots,
turnips, parsnips, swedes, celery, onions.

8 oz grated cheese.  A handful of chopped
parsley.   Jerusalem artichokes are good with this pie.

Cut the peeled vegetables into cubes.  Mix
well, boil for 5 minutes in a little salted
water.  Strain & keep the water.

Arrange the vegetables in the pie dish. Season
with salt & pepper & mix in the parsley.

With 2 oz butter, 2 oz flour and the 8 oz cheese
and vegetable water make a sauce and add
a little milk.  The sauce should be like thick
cream.    Pour over the vegetables.  Cover
with short crust pastry.  Brush with egg yolk
and milk & bake at No 7 for 35 minutes
and a further hour at No 1.

# MOUSSAKA.

One of my customers said: "I know ~ a Greek shepherd's pie"! Many recipes use minced meat but I think it tastes so much better when the meat is diced ~ quite small.

For 4 portions: 1 aubergine. A little olive oil. An onion chopped. Marjoram, salt, pepper. 2 ripe tomatoes. 1lb of cooked lamb. 1 pint of cheese sauce (p.33)

Cut the aubergine into thin slices. Brush them with oil and place oil side down in a frypan. Brush the other side and turn. Just fry them briefly. Line an oven dish with half the aubergine and save the rest for the top. In the oily pan fry the onion ~ using a little more oil if necessary. Cover and give the onion about 10 minutes. Peel and roughly chop the tomatoes. Add these and the marjoram to the onions. Add the meat. Fry for two or three minutes stirring well. Add salt and pepper to taste. Place on top of the aubergines and cover with the rest of the aubergines. Cover with the cheese sauce. Mix it in well. Bake for 50 mins at No.4.

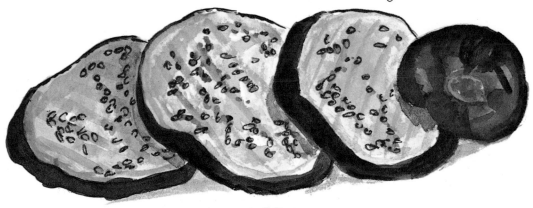

## BOEUF VINAIGRETTE

2 lbs topside cut into 2 oz slices. (The butcher will do this for you.)

1 lb onions cut into rings.

2 oz beurre manié (p.35).

Place the beef and onions in layers in a casserole finishing with a layer of onions. Sprinkle with salt and pepper and crumbled beurre manié as you arrange the layers. Cover with a tight fitting lid and cook in a low oven. (Gas Regulo 1 for 2½ hours).

Now add the vinaigrette:

2 cloves of garlic crushed.

4 anchovy fillets pounded.

3 tablespoons of olive oil. (use some anchovy oil if you like the taste)

1 tablespoon of wine vinegar.

Mix thoroughly and stir into the casserole with 2 handfuls of chopped parsley.

## PICKWICK PUDDING

1 lb suet crust: 4 oz suet (Commercial will do but fresh is always better).

1 medium grated raw potato.

½ lb self raising flour.

Salt, pepper, and a few dried herbs (thyme, parsley, marjoram).

Mix all the ingredients and add enough iced water to form into a stiff dough.

If the family are dieting use half the amount
of flour and mix with an egg instead of water, work
together well and roll out extra thin.

1lb stewing steak cut into cubes. 2oz Kidney cut small.
4oz of game (venison, guinea fowl, grouse etc) cut in dice.
this may be left over game (when available).
salt, pepper and 1 small chopped onion.
Brown stock.

Line the buttered pudding basin with the rolled
out suet crust.   Toss all the cubed ingredients in
seasoned flour (p.10)  Fill the basin.  Cover with
the stock.   Put on the lid.  Cover with two layers
of greaseproof paper and tie down well.
Cover and simmer for at least 6 hours.
~ preferably overnight.

Top of the
Basin
ie the Lid.

The collar shaped piece fits the sides

Use the
odd
pieces
for
patching

Bottom of
the
basin

A wet pastry brush is used to stick the odd pieces together.

# CHICKEN CASSEROLE ~ An Italian Recipe

3oz butter     1 cup strong chicken stock.

1 x 3lb chicken cut into 4 portions (see p. 52).

2 heaped tablespoons seasoned flour (P. 10).

Dry the chicken in the flour and fry in the butter turning constantly until brown and crisp. Put into a saucepan. Sprinkle with salt and pepper. Add a glass of red wine and simmer for 30 minutes with the lid on.

Chop an onion and crush a clove of garlic. Fry these quickly in an oz of olive oil until brown ~ about 5 minutes. Transfer to the simmering chicken trying to leave the oil in the frypan. Cut an aubergine into thin slices. Dry in seasoned flour and fry lightly in the oily pan.

Line a casserole with the aubergine slices. One or two on the bottom ~ three or four round the sides ~ and reserve two or three for the top. Put the chicken into the casserole. Cover with strips of raw green peppers and toss in a handful of green olives.

Put any seasoned flour left in the buttery/oily pan. Make a gravy with the chicken wine and stock and simmer for a few minutes. Taste and adjust the seasoning. Pour over the chicken and cover with the rest of the aubergines. Cover closely and simmer in a medium oven for about 40 mins.

This sounds complicated but is really

very easy.    It is good served with rice and cooked lettuce. (p. 18).

Peapod

Sliced carrots

Juniper

## Hand of Pork with Cream, Juniper & Rosemary

2 lbs cut from a shoulder of pork and diced.
1 cup sweet white wine or vermouth.
1 tablespoon vinegar.
½ lb sliced mushrooms.
A sprig of rosemary
8 juniper berries
1 cup of double cream
2 oz butter.
A heaped tablespoon of quick oats.

Fry the pork light brown in the butter & place in a casserole. Fry the mushrooms for a few seconds and add to the pork. Season with salt and pepper. Add the rosemary & juniper. Pour over the wine and vinegar. Sprinkle with the oats, cover and simmer in a medium oven for about 30 minutes.

Pork cooked this way is best served on a bed of rice or noodles. It tastes extremely good but looks a little dull. When the pork is tender pour over the bed of rice or pasta and, having warmed the cream pour over the whole. I like to improve the appearance by garnishing with a few bright green peas and young orange carrots.

## DR JOHNSON'S CHICKEN PUDDING.

See Pickwick pudding (p.44) for the suet crust recipe and information on lining a pudding basin with it.

1 x 3 lb chicken cut up raw into cubes. (p 52).
½ lb lean cooked gammon or ham cut into cubes.
A lot of chopped parsley and stems.
Salt and pepper.
Seasoned flour about 2 tablespoonsful (p 10).
A good sized jug of parsley sauce to serve with the pudding when it is sent to table.

Make some strong stock with the chicken bones. Toss the chicken and ham in seasoned flour and arrange in layers in the lined pudding basin sprinkling liberally with parsley and a little salt and pepper. Fill to the brim with strong chicken stock. Cover with a double layer of greaseproof paper and simmer in a closed saucepan for at least six hours.

The parsley sauce recipe is on p.30. Use half stock and half milk. This recipe was given me by a literary chef who insisted Dr Johnson ate it often!

# PIGEON PIE

4 pigeons, 1 whole onion, bouquet garni (p.5)
½ lb streaky bacon. 1 onion chopped. Some sage
Port wine. Aspic. ¼ lb Mushrooms.

Put the pigeons in a casserole with a good
lid, a whole peeled onion, a little salt and pepper
and the bouquet garni. Put into a low oven
and leave until the meat comes away easily
from the bones. This depends entirely on
the age of the pigeons!

Next day separate the meat from the
bones and arrange in layers in a pie dish.
Cover each layer with the streaky bacon lightly
grilled, a sprinkle of chopped onion and sage.
Then a few slices of the mushrooms. Sprinkle
with black pepper. Salt will not be necessary
because of the bacon. Mix the juice of the
previous cooking with an equal quantity of
port and 1½ oz of aspic. Pour over the meat
reserving some for later use. If insufficient
the discarded bones will soon make some good
stock.

Cover with short crust pastry (p.130)
Brush with an egg yolk mixed with a little
milk. Bake for 35 minutes at No 7 and
a further hour at No. 2. Good served
hot but even better eaten cold. If to be
eaten cold fill the pie after cooking with stock,
port and aspic to make the pie easier to cut.

## LASAGNE (There are many other recipes using lasagne).

This is an Italian dish shown to me by a girl from Calabria. She used lasagne (the pasta that looks like sheets of writing paper.)

1 pt white sauce with cheese.

1 lb minced beef, 1 egg, salt. pepper. oregano. thyme and a small tin tomato purée.

Garlic, chicken stock, bay leaf, sugar & basil. Parmesan cheese.

First, enough lasagne to cover a chaffing dish 4 times. These were cooked in a lot of boiling salted water for about 10 mins ~ a few at a time. Then dropped in cold water and left to drain quite separately on tea towels. Tiny meat balls were made with the minced beef. egg. salt pepper. oregano (or marjoram) and thyme. Rolled into minute balls, coated with seasoned flour and fried for a few moments in oil. A rich white sauce made of milk, butter, flour, salt, pepper & parmesan. Make a pint using 2 oz butter and 2 oz flour. Should be like double cream. A tomato sauce made of the purée, fried in oil with garlic and bay leaf and thinned with chicken stock Butter a shallow casserole or chaffing dish. Cover with lasagne. Cover with white sauce. Dot with polpetini (the meat balls) and cover thinly with tomato sauce. Repeat until the dish is nearly full ending with a layer of Lasagne, white sauce and a generous covering of the grated parmesan cheese.
Bake for 1 hour at No 4.

The LASAGNE was served with chopped, buttered spinach.

## LAMB with PEPPERS   (A South African recipe.)

I defy anyone to know that this luncheon dish is made of re-heated meat.  you will need:
½ lb onions, 1 lb tomatoes, 1 lb pimentoes.
Left over roasted lamb ~ the leg or the shoulder. cut into cubes ~ about 2 cupfuls.  Salt and pepper.
In a saucepan with a good lid melt 2 ozs butter or lamb dripping.  Fry the onion (well chopped) in this for about 10 minutes ~ (lid on, low heat). Next add the tomatoes, peeled and cut into quarters, then the pimentoes and finally the lamb.  Simmer for about 2 hours and then stir and add salt & pepper to taste.

## RAGOUT de SALPICON

This is an Italian shepherd's pie ~ specially useful for use with new potatoes. It is made of:
Minced left over meat (chicken, pork or tongue)
Raw new potatoes cut like crisps but a bit thicker
Tomato sauce (see the Lasagne recipe opposite).
Grated cheese.  English hard cheese is good for this.  Butter a chafing dish.  Make about three layers starting with meat covered with sauce, then potatoes covered with cheese.  Cook for 1 hour at No 4.  The top potatoes should be crisp & golden-brown.
salt & pepper the potato layers.

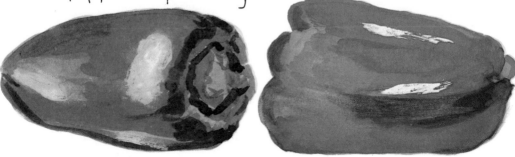

# How to Cut up a Raw 3lb Chicken

Pull out the wings and cut off the first two joints (for the stock pot) and leave the wing looking like the illustration in figure 3.

1

2

Lay the bird on it's side and cut under the thigh and leg taking these right off and then separating them as shown in figure 2.

Cut off the leg end for the stock pot.

Finally cut away the breast from both sides as shown in figure 3

The carcass and oddments make the best chicken stock.

3

# CHAPTER THREE
## VEGETABLES

Two basic rules when cooking vegetables in boiling water: 1. Plants that grow above the earth, high heat, lid off and very quick cooking. 2. Roots that grow beneath the soil, low heat, lid on and long slow cooking.

Never salt the water until it is boiling. It takes longer and uses more heat to boil salted water than plain water -

### Shallots, Onions or Chives?

Shallots have a better flavour than onions and they do seem to be more digestible. However they are often difficult to buy and onions may always be used instead. Chives used in salads are better than onion or shallots.

In the winter when chives are dormant stored onions sometimes start sending up green shoots. These can be cut like chives and used as a tasty garnish. Leeks used raw and cut fine are also useful for this job.

### Broad Beans.

These are delicious cooked whole in their pods; or sliced like runner beans. This is only possible if they are home grown as they have to be picked very, very, young. Sometimes they need a pinch of bi-carbonate when the water is salted to keep their bright green colour.

# PURPLE SPROUTING BROCCOLI

Choose a saucepan that just fits the length of the broccoli heads and stems. Put them in and just cover with water. Take them out and bring the water to the boil. Salt and add the broccoli. When the pot returns to boiling point allow 8 minutes. This should leave the broccoli very bright green and tender~ though still needing eating! With practice there is no need to measure the water as you will judge the correct amount. Alternatively put the broccoli in the saucepan and pour on boiling water from a kettle. This is very convenient when entertaining but more extravagant on the heating bills.

Best, I think, served with melted butter like asparagus. However it is good as a vegetable accompaniment to a meat dish and can be served plain, with Hollandaise, Béchamel or cheese sauce.

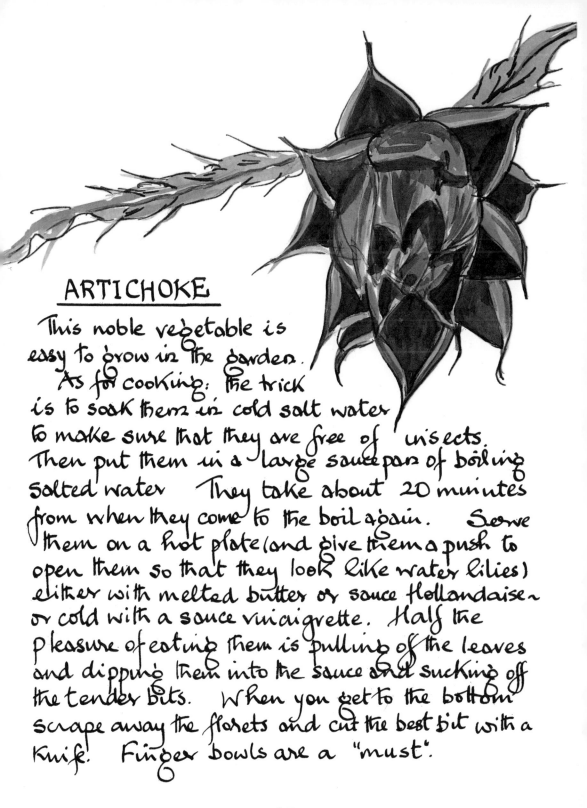

## ARTICHOKE

This noble vegetable is
easy to grow in the garden.
     As for cooking: the trick
is to soak them in cold salt water
to make sure that they are free of insects.
Then put them in a large saucepan of boiling
salted water. They take about 20 minutes
from when they come to the boil again.   Serve
them on a hot plate (and give them a push to
open them so that they look like water lilies)
either with melted butter or sauce Hollandaise
or cold with a sauce vinaigrette. Half the
pleasure of eating them is pulling of the leaves
and dipping them into the sauce and sucking off
the tender bits.   When you get to the bottom
scrape away the florets and cut the best bit with a
knife.   Finger bowls are a "must".

~55~

# RUNNER BEANS

Of all our British Vegetables
this is surely one of our very best.
If they are not freshly picked
from the garden it is a good thing
to top & tail them and cut away
any stringy bits and soak them for
an hour in cold water. This
makes them stiff and crisp and
far easier to slice.     If they are
young and freshly gathered
from the garden they only
need eight minutes' boiling.
     They are very good
          just broken into
               about 2" lengths
                    if really young.
If they are fresh    and correctly
cooked they should squeak on
the teeth ~ as newly washed hair
does when it is thoroughly
rinsed clean.     Serve with
a nice little lump of butter.
     With curry they go well as
a side dish tossed in a little
of the spiced sauce.

# FRENCH BEANS

These are very good but never quite have the flavour of the runner bean. They are just topped and tailed. If small they can be cooked whole. If larger they can be snapped in two and this makes it easier to remove any strings. They usually cook tender in boiling salted water in about 6 to 8 minutes and should be strained and topped with a knob of butter. A pleasant variation is to cook a few rashers of streaky bacon which have been cut very small until crisp and the fat has run out.

Cook the beans the usual way and having strained them toss them for a few seconds in the bacon pan and then pour them, bacon and all, into a hot dish. Cooked this way they are good as an entrée ~ or served with chicken, pork or veal.

Delicious as a salad, boiled and tossed in french dressing.

# SUGAR PEAS

Are excellent cooked as
if they are garden peas. Just
top and tail them and cook
in salted boiling water (with
or without a sprig of fresh
mint) until tender ~
usually they take between 6
and 8 minutes. Put a
knob of butter with them
in a warmed serving dish.
However, I prefer them the
way my Belgian Grandmother cooked them.
You need:       1lb of Sugar Peas (6 servings)
                1 small chopped onion.
                2oz butter.
                The outside leaves of a lettuce.
                A bundle of young carrots.

   Melt the butter in a medium sized saucepan with a good lid. Add the chopped onion
and simmer for 10 minutes ( low heat, lid on)
Stir, then add the lettuce leaves just wet
from being washed and the young carrots scraped,
but whole. On top put the pea pods. Sprinkle
with a little salt and cover closely. Cook on
a very low heat for about 40 minutes. They

should be tender but slightly discoloured. Stir, then add a dessertspoonful of beurre manié to thicken the natural juices. Add freshly milled black pepper. Serve in a hot dish with all the pan juices. With a hot boiled bacon joint pois mange-tout cooked thus are a feast for the gods.

They are also very good as an hors d'oeuvres or salad tossed in french dressing. Fresh chopped mint can be added if liked.

## ELDER STEMS
Young thick green stems can be peeled in spring cut into thin rounds and added to green salad.

## RATATOUILLE.
A mixture of Auberguies, Courgettes, Tomatoes, Pimentoes – the green ones, olive oil, garlic & onion.

Crush a clove of garlic, chop an onion and fry them in about 2 tablespoons of olive oil. Stir for 2 or 3 minutes. Now add a pimiento, chopped, an aubergine & two courgettes, chopped, and fry in the mixture. Finally peel 3 or 4 tomatoes, cut up roughly and stir in. Add salt and pepper and simmer for about 30 minutes with the lid on. Overcooking makes it go into a mush. Pimentoes take the most cooking. When they taste "done" it is ready.

<u>Kohl Rabi</u> is not nearly
well enough known. It
looks rather like a turnip,
but the root grows above the
ground.  When first
I grew them in the garden
my husband ~ who with
our son was reading "Eagle"
each week ~ decided that
they had landed from another
planet.

Just peel and dice them and
cook in boiling salted water
until tender ~ about 12 to
15 minutes.  They can be
served with a good knob
of butter; white sauce, plain
or with grated nutmeg added.
They are delicious in cheese
sauce.  If done with
cheese I like to cover them
with the sauce, sprinkle
with a generous topping
of grated cheese and then
grill them until golden
brown.

Purple roots or white roots
are both equally delicious.

BRUSSELS SPROUTS are the delight of some and anathema to the rest. I had a sister-in-law who had an American mother. She had heard Americans say: "Great Britain! that's where they pretend they like eating Brussels sprouts ~" They need the minimum of preparation. Taking off the outer leaves is quite unnecessary unless they are damaged and the practice of cutting crosses in their bottoms is probably a good Christian custom but otherwise needless.       Put the sprouts into boiling salted water + add a similar amount of sugar.    When they come to the boil again time them for 8 minutes.   Strain and press well to remove excess water. Put into a hot dish and top with a good knob of butter ~ nutty flavoured and delicious.

Another way is to place the cooked sprouts into a horizontal rotary cutting machine.   Add cream and re-heat in a buttery pan.   It is extraordinary how this alters their flavour.   Confirmed Brussels sprouts haters have really enjoyed them; of course they didn't know they were Brussels sprouts ~ ~ ~

# Aubergine (Brinjal or Egg plant)

Aubergines should be cut into slices and sprinkled with salt.* After an hour if wiped clean the bitterness is gone. They can be fried in butter and oil or dipped into batter and fried in vegetable oil. I like to cook them whole in boiling water ~ test with a pointed skewer ~ when this goes in easily put a cloth in the colander and pour the aubergine in. Tie up and squeeze out the water. Turn into a hot dish and mash with a fork, or a potato masher. Add olive oil, salt and freshly milled black pepper.

They are at their best in the Greek dish: Moussaka. The recipe for this is on page 43. Also very good in Ratatouille (p. 59).

\* I don't bother!

# PARSNIP

Being a sweet vegetable it is
not always liked. However, peeled,
cut into quite small fingers, simmered
tender and tossed in melted butter
it is a useful winter vegetable.
("Flattery will butter no parsnips!")

Roasted around the joint
it goes well with roasted beef and is
available when other fresh vegetables
are in short supply

I like it best served with
bacon. The bacon is grilled. The
parsnips (already simmered tender)
are then browned in the bacon fat.

Parsnips are good as one of
the vegetables used in the pie on
page 42.

# JERUSALEM ARTICHOKES

The recipe for Jerusalem artichoke
soup is on page 19.. They are a useful
component of the vegetable pie on page 42.

However they are not so well known
as artichoke crisps. Scrub them but
do not bother to peel. Cut them very
thin and fry in deep fat or oil until
they are crisp. Toss with salt in
kitchen paper + serve.

# CELERY

This is a wonderfully versatile vegetable; equally good raw or cooked. It makes a delicious salad chopped up in equal quantity with raw cooking apple and tossed in french dressing.

It is a quick and easy vegetable cut into short lengths, boiled for about 10 minutes and served with a knob of butter. It is one of the good natured vegetables served braised (p. 164). It is an essential ingredient for Pink Salad (p. 74.)

Probably it is best served as an accompaniment with Stilton cheese. It makes a good cocktail snack cut into 2" lengths and filled with cream cheese.

Tinned hearts of celery are a pleasant alternative to chicory in the recipe using ham (p. 75)

CELERIAC ~ the turnip shaped celery root can be used grated in salads or cut into cubes and boiled. It cooks quite quickly. I like it best covered with cheese sauce and grilled.

~ 64 ~

# CAULIFLOWER

is the slimmer's friend.
It scarcely counts on
many diet sheets.
I like to keep the
young green
leaves and
cook these
too. Cut
off the florets
and then
cut the large
centre stem
into tiny dice.
When salted water
is boiling rapidly; put in
the leaves and stem and give them a couple
of minutes start and then add the florets. They
take about 6 more minutes. Best with butter ~
but if a cheese sauce is liked ~ or a white sauce ~
use half milk and half water to make either.

The florets raw ~ cut small and soaked in
French dressing make a good crunchy salad.
Left over cooked florets make a good salad
in equal quantities of cream, mayonnaise and
tomato ketchup with a dash of brandy.

# Pimentoes ~

It is not often that pimentoes are served as a vegetable. They are nearly always in a dish such as piperade Basque or lamb with peppers (p51).

I like them as an entrée when serving fish as the main dish. Vegetables don't go well with fish.

Cut the peppers into six long pieces, taking out the seeds. If possible choose red, orange and green ones and cook for about 8 minutes in boiling salted water. Strain and put in a buttered chaffing dish. The assortment of colours looks attractive. Make a cheese sauce using the water they were cooked in with 1oz of butter and 1oz flour and 3oz cheddar cheese. Pour over and grill a golden brown. Good served with brown bread and butter.

They add taste to green salads sliced very thin and added raw.

## SEAKALE BEET
### Swiss Chard or
### Bette ~

This vegetable is such good value ~ two for the price of one. The green leaves cook like spinach. The stems make another dish. They are good boiled until tender (about 10 minutes) and then served with butter, or a white sauce ~ or cheese sauce. I like them cold as a salad served with French dressing. If they are intended as a salad they should be left long. The spinach part cooks green and tender in about 4 minutes. A tablespoonful of water will cook a large dish-ful. Exception to the rule! Lid on.

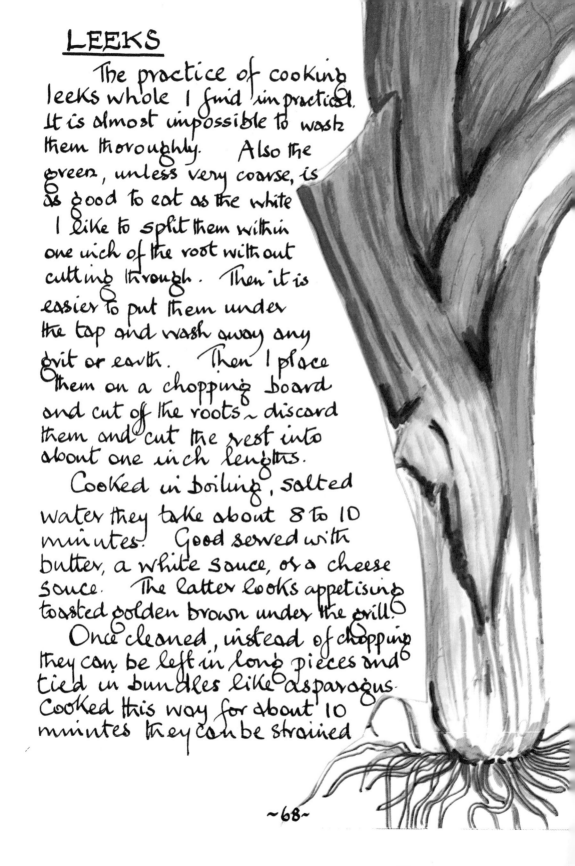

# LEEKS

The practice of cooking leeks whole I find impractical. It is almost impossible to wash them thoroughly.    Also the green, unless very coarse, is as good to eat as the white

I like to split them within one inch of the root without cutting through. Then it is easier to put them under the tap and wash away any grit or earth.    Then I place them on a chopping board and cut of the roots ~ discard them and cut the rest into about one inch lengths.

Cooked in boiling, salted water they take about 8 to 10 minutes.   Good served with butter, a white sauce, or a cheese sauce.   The latter looks appetising toasted golden brown under the grill.

Once cleaned, instead of chopping they can be left in long pieces and tied in bundles like asparagus. Cooked this way for about 10 minutes they can be strained

chilled and served with a sauce vinaigrette.
    Leeks are good cooked without water. For
4 good helpings you need:
    1 medium sized onion (chopped).
    4 leeks washed and cut into inch lengths.
    6 young carrots cut into rings.
    1 oz of butter or oil.
Start the onion in the melted butter in a
saucepan with a good lid.    Cook very gently.
10 minutes should soften the onion and start
the gooey mixture off.    Put in the carrots and
leeks and a little salt ~ not too much as you are
not going to throw anything away. Now put
the lid on, make the heat as gentle as possible
and "forget" the dish.   When tender the vegetable
is ready.
    This is a good-tempered vegetable. It can
be reheated without anyone detecting any
change in the flavour.    It will sit for hours
in a covered casserole at the bottom of the
oven if the family are later than expected.

# COURGETTES

They can be baked whole wrapped in silver foil.      Or cut in rings and fried with butter and olive oil in a pan.   Cook gently and turn when they are golden brown.      They are good cut into four long strips and boiled in salt water ~ about 8 minutes ~ then press them in a colander and add butter and chopped parsley.

They make a good hors d'oeuvres cut in rings, left raw and tossed in mayonnaise.

My favourite way is to cut them into dice ~ cook with a chopped onion in butter in a closed pan very gently until tender. Then sprinkle them with grated cheese and chopped chives. Stir in a tablespoon of yoghourt and serve.

Cooked this way they are good with grilled gammon. Also delicious cooked as the young marrow on page 73.

# Turnips & Swedes

are the only vegetables I can think of that need thick peeling. I have sliced through this Swede to show you the outer case which is bitter. This often puts people off them as they remember bitter, watery, stringy things from school days!

1 lb of each peeled thick, diced and boiled tender are delicious mixed with a bundle of chopped watercress and a nice dollop of cream. This is a good natured vegetable which will sit almost indefinitely at the bottom of the oven.

Either Turnips or Swedes are quite excellent with shoulder of lamb (Recipe on page 105).

They also make a good astringent vegetable mashed with plenty of salt, pepper and butter with a rich dish such as loin of pork.

They are one of the ingredients suitable for the Vegetable and cheese pie given on page 42.

## THE VEGETABLE MARROW ~ quite the

most misunderstood fruit I know. It should not be an entrant for a Vegetable Show ~ it should be young and tender ~ a finger nail should go into it easily. When really young before the seeds form their hard shells it can be cooked skin, pips and all. Also as it is probably 90% water it shouldn't be cooked in more water.

My favourite way is:

A young marrow diced.

A small onion chopped.

1 oz dripping, butter or oil.

2 large tomatoes peeled and quartered.

Simmer the onion in the fat for 10 minutes ~ take off the lid and put in the tomato ~ cook briskly for a few minutes stirring well ~ then add the marrow and a little salt. Cover closely and simmer for about 30 minutes.

Marrow is delicious cooked thus and

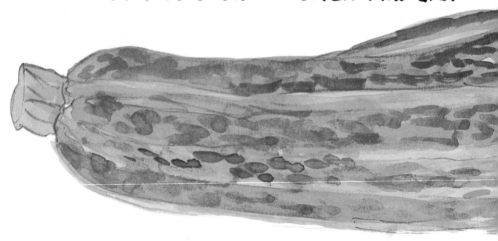

after serving reserve the natural juice and any marrow left over to make a delicious soup. (p.14)

Marrow Fritters.    I was shown how to make these by a young Calabrian girl. Cut the marrow through in ¼" slices. Sprinkle with salt and leave for a little while. Wipe off the salt and dry with a little flour.    Dip in a thin batter and fry in oil in a shallow pan for 2 or 3 minutes. Turn and continue frying until tender ~ about 5 minutes. Drain on Kitchen paper and serve at once.

Batter   4oz plain flour
         1egg, salt and a gill of milk.
         Mix and thin with water.

Better for being
left standing
before use.

~73~

## CHICORY.

This excellent vegetable has many uses. It is good cut in rings and made into:

PINK SALAD (My English Grand-mother's recipe).

1 cooked beetroot, diced.
An equal quantity of chopped celery and chicory cut in rings.
A teaspoon of chopped chives.
Mix well with real mayonnaise.
The beetroot sends it an attractive pink. The sweet beetroot, crunchy celery and bitter chicory make a delicious mixture. Very good served with ham.

Chicory can be cut in half lengthwise and then halved again lengthwise. Fry in butter or bacon fat until hot but not really cooked. Very good served with grilled gammon.

Braised whole in a casserole at the bottom of the oven with a lot of butter and a squeeze of lemon juice it becomes one of the good natured vegetables that will simmer indefinitely without spoiling or be re-heated without loss of quality.

Chicons can be pulled apart and mixed with lettuce in a green salad

Chicory and Orange is another good salad. Cut the chicons into rings and mix with slices of peeled orange. Dress with French dressing using orange juice instead of vinegar or lemon.

This salad goes well with cold duck or goose.

**Chicory & Carrots** is another of the good-natured vegetables.

Fry a small chopped onion in butter (lid on, low heat, 20 minutes). Cut carrots into rings and put them on top of the onions. Cover the saucepan and simmer for another 20 minutes, shaking now and then. Finally put an equal quantity of chicory cut into rings and simmer for as long as you like ~ or transfer to a casserole and forget it at the bottom of the oven. This will re-heat without spoiling. The sweet carrots and bitter chicory compliment eachother and make a new taste. Good served with chicken or veal.

### Chicory with Ham. (6 portions)

Fry 6 whole chicons in a closed frypan with butter for about 5 minutes to soften them a little. When cool enough to handle wrap each chicon in a thin slice of ham and put into a buttered chaffing dish. Cover with a cheese sauce made half of milk and half vegetable water (white wine if it is an occasion) 1 oz butter, 1 oz flour and 4 oz grated cheddar cheese. Bake for 1 hour at No. 2. If a browner top is liked finish off under the grill. If you use wine make the sauce with milk and do not add the wine until the flour is cooked.

# ASPARAGUS
Surely the queen of vegetables.
It is probably at it's very
best in May boiled and served
with melted butter. 10 minutes
should be time enough to get
the tips tender. After all you are
not meant to eat all the stem
~ although I usually do!
   A Belgian sauce as an alternative
is a mixture of 4 oz melted butter
and a hard boiled egg chopped
very fine. Some prefer it with
<u>Hollandaise Sauce</u>
2 tablespoons wine vinegar boiled to
         reduce by half and let cool.
Put in a double sauce pan and whisk
in 2 egg yolks over boiling water.
When it starts to thicken whisk
in 4 oz butter cut into cubes. When
all is absorbed take away from
the heat and season with salt,
pepper & lemon juice.
   Cold Asparagus is excellent
either with mayonnaise or
French dressing
   It is even good tinned and
this is used in the Quiche (p144).

# CHAPTER FOUR
## Sugar & Spice
### (written in the Seychelles)

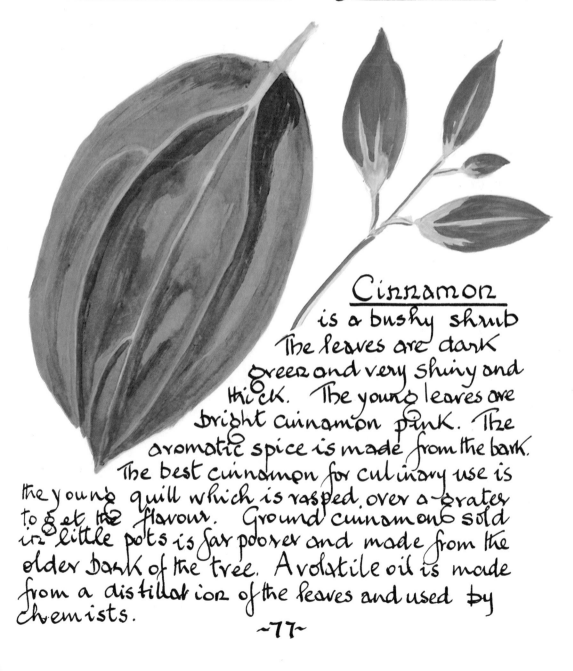

### Cinnamon

is a bushy shrub
The leaves are dark
green and very shiny and
thick. The young leaves are
bright cinnamon pink. The
aromatic spice is made from the bark.
The best cinnamon for culinary use is
the young quill which is rasped over a grater
to get the flavour. Ground cinnamons sold
in little pots is far poorer and made from the
older bark of the tree. A volatile oil is made
from a distillation of the leaves and used by
chemists.

# Cinnamon Biscuits (splendid with coffee)

½ lb plain flour. ¼ lb butter ¼ lb demerara sugar.
1 egg. Grated cinnamon. Some almonds.

Cream the butter & sugar. Add the egg. Mix well.
Sift in the flour. Stir. Grate cinnamon over the
entire surface until lightly covered. Mix
thoroughly and roll thin. Cut into biscuits
decorating each one with half a blanched almond.

Cook on a buttered paper in a tin for about
10 minutes at No. 5.

## Pear Chutney

2 lbs wind falls (Pears, apples, plums mixed).
1 pt good malt vinegar. 1 lb demerara sugar. Ground
cloves (coffee grinder does this well). Rasped cinnamon
Cayenne pepper.          Peel & cut the fruit roughly.
Pour over the vinegar and sugar. Simmer until
tender. Put the strained fruit in a jar and reduce
the liquid boiling rapidly for about 10 minutes.
Taste and season with cloves, cinnamon and
cayenne.     Pour over the fruit and cover closely.
This is an excellent alternative to expensive mango
chutney.

## Lemon or Lime Curd.

½ lb sugar. 2 oz butter. 2 eggs. 1 lemon or 2 limes.
In the inner part of a double saucepan melt the butter.
pour in the fruit juice & add the sugar. Grate in the
citron peel. Beat the eggs. Put the inner into the
outer container full of boiling water. Add the eggs
and stir until the mixture thickens. It is far
thicker when cold. Keeps in a jar in the fridge
for up to six weeks.

## VANILLA

Wild vanilla is a beautiful white orchid. There appear to be no leaves ~ just the fleshy green stems and lovely white flowers followed by the green rather French bean like pods. These in the cultivated form become the delicious aromatic spice. This orchid has an insignificant flower and thick straplike leaves and has to have a "host" tree to cling to.

Vanilla pods should live in a jar of caster sugar. Their perfume flavours the sugar & can be used again and again.

Vanille sauvage

Vanilla essence is a distillation of cloves and not allowed in my house. Milk for puddings can be boiled with a pod in. The pod is then washed, dried & put back in it's sugar pot. They last for months.

## SHORTBREAD

8oz plain flour. 5oz butter 3oz Vanilla sugar.

Mix together and when like fine crumbs pour into a baking tin. Flatten to a uniform thickness. Bake at No.3 for 20 minutes. Leave in the hot oven for 20 minutes. Cut while still hot into biscuits and leave to cool before removing from the tin.

# CLOVES

A clove bud
picked immature
ready for drying.

    The clove tree is tall but dainty
and the leaves are evergreen, dark and
shiny like a laurel.    The perfume of
the tree is very strong and usually you
detect the scent before you recognise
the shape.
    Cloves as we know them, are the
immature buds which are picked and
dried. If left these open into white blossom
and mature into waxy, pink fruits.
    Cloves freshly ground are so

much better than the powdered variety that I like to keep a small pepper mill specially for grinding them. Any savoury pork recipe into which a few grinds of fresh clove is added has a piquancy quite different and most appetising.

## OLD FASHIONED PORK BRAWN

½ pig's head, salt, cloves, mace, pepper. 1 onion. 1 carrot. 1 stick celery.

Put the head in a saucepan with a handful of salt and cover with water. Bring to the boil then remove from the heat. When cool enough to handle take out the head and throw away the liquid. Clean the saucepan and start again.

Now put the head back with the onion, carrot and celery all roughly chopped. Cover with boiling water and when it boils again add a dessertspoonful of salt. Simmer for about 2 hours. The meat should come away from the bone easily. When cool enough to handle separate the meat from the bone and chop roughly. Put in a basin or a mould and season to taste with the pepper, freshly ground cloves and mace.

Any unattractive pieces can go back in the stock pot ~ or the dog bowl! Reduce the stock by rapid boiling until it is about ¼ of the quantity. Pour a little into the mould, put on a saucer and a 4lb weight and leave to cool.

# RECIPES FOR NUTMEG & MACE

## A sauce for shell fish.

1oz butter. 1oz plain flour
¼ pt of white wine and fish stock mixed.
1 tablespoon double cream.
A pinch of mace. Salt and pepper to taste.
Make a roux with the butter, flour and liquid.
Add the mace, salt and pepper. Stir in the cream
and remove from the heat. This sauce is a
beautiful additive to left over white fish and shell
fish. The fish and sauce can be poured into a
flame proof dish, sprinkled with fresh breadcrumbs,
grated cheese and dabbed with butter. Grill until
bubbling and an attractive colour, sprinkle with
chopped parsley and serve. Fresh haddock and
lobster or prawns cooked this way are very good.
They can be done in ramekin dishes or scallop
shells.

## NUTMEG

Nutmeg is good on a plain junket. First pour
on a little cream and then sprinkle with the spice.
Page 60 gives a recipe for nutmeg sauce with Kohl Rabbi.

Nutmeg, mace and cinnamon together give
an eastern flavour to homely dishes like green
tomato chutney. Mace is good with boiled
white cabbage. Add melted butter and a
pinch of mace when cooked.

# Nutmeg
## with it's covering of Mace

Mace

Nut meg

" I had a little nut tree and
Nothing would it bear
But a silver nutmeg
And a golden pear ~ "
Now, at last, I understand this nursery jingle.
The nutmeg tree is quite a large bush ~
about 20 ft high. The leaves are evergreen
and very shiny and amongst the branches
hang the golden pears. Open them up
and you find the crimson mace surrounding
the money crop of the "silver" meg.

# PICKLING VEGETABLES

Pickled vegetables have to be brined.

½ lb of salt to 4 pts water. Bring to the boil and strain through a cloth. When cold it is ready for use.

A good mustard pickle:

1 lb of cucumber cut in wide rounds + cut in four
1 lb of small onions or shallots (peeled).
1 cauliflower - the florets only cut small.
Put the vegetables in the brine and leave for 24 hrs.
Cover with a heavy plate so that they are held underneath the brine.

3 pints vinegar (good malt is best).
3 oz demerara sugar.
2 oz dry mustard.
1 oz tumeric.
1 oz salt.

Bring the vinegar & the sugar to the boil. Keep back a small quantity of vinegar to smooth the mustard & tumeric & add this to the vinegar and the salt. Stir to avoid lumps.

Strain the brined vegetables and put into the pickle. Simmer for 10 minutes and bottle in hot jars.

Makesure the bottles are well sealed. Loose covers mean waste by evaporation and can cause mould and mildew.

This pickle is ready for use in a week but improves greatly for longer maturing.

Runner beans in short lengths can be used in this recipe.

Cauliflower florets    Pickling onions    and    Cut Cucumber

## GREEN TOMATO CHUTNEY.

4 lbs green tomatoes sliced. Leave tiny ones whole.

½ lb onions peeled & sliced.

½ lb ripe red pimentoes (Seeded & cut in squares)

1 oz salt.

Mix well in an earthenware crock or glass bowl
    and leave overnight.

2 pts good malt vinegar

1 lb demerara sugar. Mix together & bring to the boil.

Add ½ lb currants, ½ lb sultanas, & ½ lb prunes. The
    prunes should be soaked overnight & cut from their stones.

Add ½ pt of stem ginger in it's syrup (chopped or liquidized).

1 teaspoon cayenne pepper.

Now add the tomatoes & onions etc to this brew
and simmer until it thickens.    Stir often or
it will burn.

This is an extravagant recipe but it really
tastes like chutney that our grandmothers made.

## POPPADUMS.

    Poppadums are delicious with curries
and spiced food. The secret of frying them
crisp is to use a pan of oil about ¾" deep and
just below boiling point. Put in, turn, and drain.

# Rum Butter

To serve with Christmas pudding & mince pies.

½ lb soft butter.
½ lb soft brown sugar.
1 glass rum.
1 egg yolk. grated nutmeg. icing sugar.

Beat the egg yolk, sugar & rum for 10 minutes on an electric beater. Add the very soft butter and beat until white. Sprinkle with grated nutmeg and icing sugar. Be careful not to over-heat the butter.

# Spiced Fish (A recipe from the Seychelles)

For 6 portions a 4 lb fish. It should be whole but gutted. Hake, Mullet, fresh haddock, Bass or pollack. It needs to be a plump meaty fish.
1 clove garlic - crushed - 1 fresh chilli (optional)
1 teaspoon of Turmeric, Curry & ground ginger.
1 dessertspoon vegetable cooking oil.
choose a fire proof dish that can do from oven to table. Butter this well - put in the fish-score the skin diagonally & rub in the garlic, oil, and spices. Cover with silver foil and bake for 30 minutes at No. 7.

While the fish is cooking make the sauce:
1 onion chopped & simmered in oil until cooked but not coloured. 1 clove garlic crushed, 1 green pepper seeded & cut in strips, ½ lb peeled tomatoes (tinned may be used) 1 stem ginger sliced and a little of its syrup, 1 glass white wine, salt & pepper. Simmer all together.

Pour over the fish & serve with rice.
If it is impossible to buy fresh chillies use cayenne.

~ 86 ~

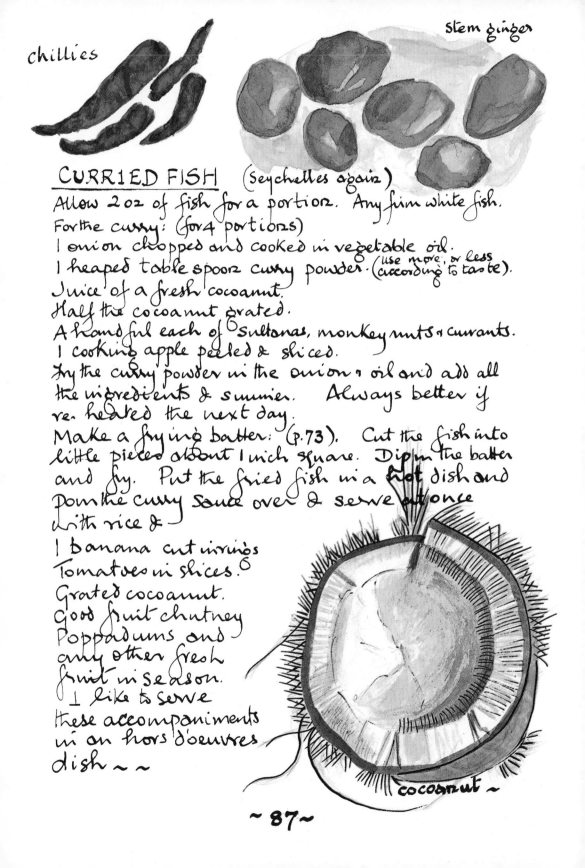

chillies

stem ginger

## CURRIED FISH (Seychelles again)

Allow 2 oz of fish for a portion. Any firm white fish.
For the curry: (for 4 portions)
1 onion chopped and cooked in vegetable oil.
1 heaped table spoon curry powder. (use more, or less according to taste).
Juice of a fresh cocoanut.
Half the cocoanut grated.
A handful each of sultanas, monkey nuts & currants.
1 cooking apple peeled & sliced.
Fry the curry powder in the onion, oil and add all
the ingredients & simmer.    Always better if
re-heated the next day.
Make a frying batter: (p.73).    Cut the fish into
little pieces about 1 inch square. Dip in the batter
and fry.  Put the fried fish in a hot dish and
pour the curry sauce over & serve at once
with rice &
1 banana cut in rings
Tomatoes in slices.
Grated cocoanut.
Good fruit chutney
Poppadums and
any other fresh
fruit in season.
I like to serve
these accompaniments
in an hors d'oeuvres
dish ~~

cocoanut ~

# CURRIED LAMB (A Kenya recipe)

1 lb Lamb (shoulder suitable raw or cooked. Raw is better)
2 onions chopped & cooked in butter (lid on, low heat, 20 mins)
2 large cooking apples (peeled & sliced).
1 fresh cocoanut (the milk for stock - the flesh grated - half in the curry - the other half as a garnish)
2 tablespoons curry powder (or 1 of powder & 1 of paste)
1 tablespoon fruit syrup (from any tinned fruit)
1 tablespoon syrup from mango chutney.
1 tablespoon sultanas.  I also add a tablespoon Garam masala.
1 teaspoon chopped mint.  salt.  butter.

When the onion is tender fry in the curry powder and/or paste for 2 or 3 minutes.  Then fry in the lamb which has been cut into little cubes.  Then add all the rest of the ingredients. When it is simmering well make a fresh pot of Indian tea and pour in about 3/4 pint.

Curry should be simmered for at least 2 hours. It is always better if kept until the next day and re-heated.

To taste for the strength of the brew put a little on a tiny piece of hot buttered toast.  If not hot enough fry more curry powder or paste in butter and add to the dish.

Serve with rice & fruits as in the previous recipe.

## MILD CHICKEN CURRY.    (A recipe from Malaya).

1 chicken is enough for 4 portions.
Cut the meat~ leaving the legs on the bones.
Make strong stock with the rest of the carcass.
Fry 4 onions chopped in 4 oz butter.
Fry in curry paste & powder ~ about 1 tablespoon.
Fry in the chicken meat. Add the milk of a
cocoanut, some shredded cocoanut and 3 cups
of strong chicken stock. Add salt and a teaspoon~
ful of thyme & parsley (better fresh & chopped but
dry may be used).    (Garam-masala improves this recipe).
    Simmer for at least an hour. Again better
served the next day after re-heating.


    Serve with: Fried bananas, Rings of
hard boiled egg, french beans & rice.
Poppadums, grated cocoanut and mango
chutney should also accompany this dish.
The french beans should be mixed with a little
curry sauce.

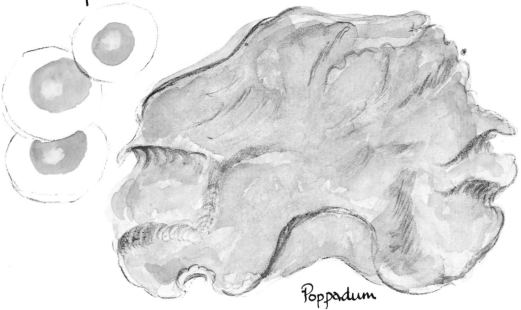

Poppadum

# CHAPTER FIVE    FISH

## LOBSTER au GRATIN

This recipe lends itself to any shellfish or a mixture of shellfish and white fish. This makes 4 generous portions or 6-8 for use as an entrée.

1 lb lobster meat. 2 peeled sliced tomatoes. 1 egg ~ hard boiled and sliced ~ 1 teaspoon dry mustard. 2 oz cheddar cheese grated. 1 dessertspoon grated parmesan, 1 pinch mace.

Put the lobster, tomatoes, and egg in layers in a buttered fire-proof dish. Cover with thick cheese sauce. For the sauce 1 oz butter, 1 oz flour, ¼ pt milk, 1 cup of white wine, salt and pepper & mace.

Melt the butter, fry in the flour, add the milk and wine gradually ~ lastly the cheddar cheese. Season with salt and pepper. Bring to the boil. Pour over the dish. Sprinkle with the parmesan.

Place under the grill until all is bubbling and the top attractively browned.

## LOBSTER NEWBURG

Split the lobster lengthways. Clean the stomach from the head. Take out the meat from the body and the claws and cut it into little pieces. Fry in 1 oz butter and add a tablespoon of sherry and a tablespoon of double cream. Take off the heat and stir in an egg yolk. Season with salt, pepper & nutmeg. Replace in the half shells. Cover with grated cheese, Grill until bubbling and golden brown.

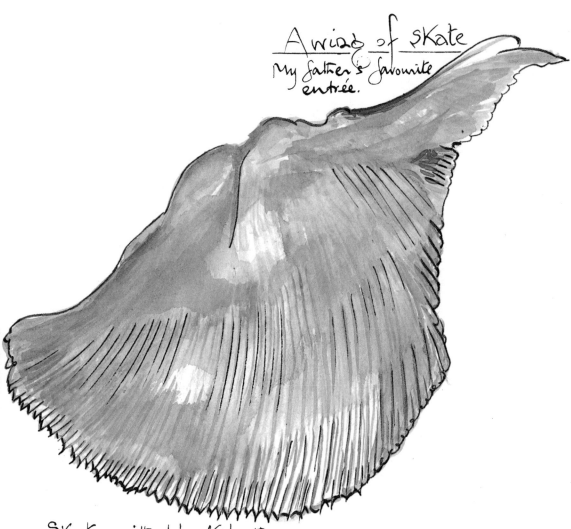

# A wing of skate
My father's favourite entrée.

## Skate with black butter

1 wing of skate per portion. salt black pepper
Butter. lemon juice or vinegar, chopped parsley
Chicken stock.

Simmer the wing in chicken stock (about 10 mins)
Fry together 1 oz butter, 1 dessert spoon lemon or
vinegar. Cook the butter till it starts to brown
then add the vinegar or lemon. Put the fish on a hot
dish. Sprinkle with salt & pepper. Pour over
the black butter and sprinkle with parsley.

## CRAB RUMBLE TUMBLE     For 4 Portions

Serve either in scallop shells or on buttered toast.

1 oz butter
4 eggs.
2 oz brown crab meat
2 oz white crab meat
Salt, black pepper &
cayenne.

Melt the butter and fry the brown meat with salt, freshly ground black pepper and a little cayenne. Scramble in the eggs. Lastly toss in the white meat & serve at once decorated with water cress.

## CRAB PANCAKES     For 4 substantial portions

6 oz white & 6 oz brown crabmeat. 1 pt of cheese sauce (p.33)
Cayenne pepper, 1 oz vinegar, 1 slice brown bread crumbs.
4 thin pancakes. (These quantities will make 8 pancakes served as an entrée).

Mix crab meats, ½ sauce, vinegar, cayenne, bread crumbs & salt.
Divide into 4 and fill the pancakes. Place in a well buttered chafing dish and cover with the rest of the sauce thinned with a little white wine.
Bake for 10 minutes at No 4 then finish under the grill.

## DEVONSHIRE HAKE     A Norwegian recipe.

A 4lb hake. Put this in a fish kettle ~ or souce-
pan large enough to take it. 1 onion roughly cut.
a sprig of fennel, a bay leaf, ½ a lemon (skin and
all) salt and pepper. Carefully pour in just enough
boiling water barely to cover the fish. Simmer for
10 minutes ~ don't let it boil. Keep the lid on and
let the fish cool in the water.

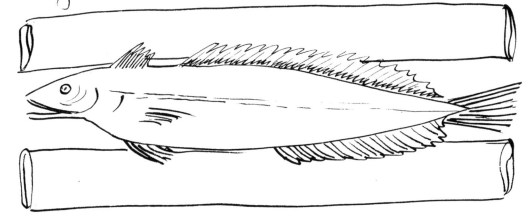

This is the tricky bit. Get the fish on to the
dish you are going to serve it on. It is easy with a
fish kettle. Some people cook it wrapped in net curtaining
and get it out that way. Place folded greaseproof
paper either side of the fish. Trim away fins with sharp
scissors. Take off the top two fillets and flip them
over on to the greaseproof paper. Lift out the bone.

Decorate one underside with prawn sauce (p.31) and
the other with mushroom sauce (p.30). Now pick up
the paper either end & keeping it taut flip the top
fillets back. Use the rest of the sauces to cover the fish
being careful to get the mushroom top over the under
side prawn and vice versa. A splendid dish for
summer entertaining served with hot new potatoes
and green salad.

## FISHPUDDING (A Norwegian recipe).

Cut a lb of fish fillets (almost any white fish is suitable~ halibut is very good) into pieces and put them into the liquidizer with a cup of single cream, 2 eggs, 2 tablespoons potato flour and a little freshly grated nutmeg. Blend for about 2 minutes. Add 2 tablespoons milk and 2 tablespoons dry white vermouth and a cup of double cream. Pour into a buttered mould. Place the mould in a shallow pan of water and bake at No 4 for an hour. Turn out on to a dish and decorate with shelled lobster claws or prawns just tossed in a fry pan with hot butter to warm them. Serve with <u>sour cream fennel sauce</u>: Beat a cup of sour cream until it thickens and add a tablespoon of chopped fennel. Heat in a double saucepan and serve at once. Fresh cream can be soured with a few drops of lemon juice.

# Salmon

Salmon is very good served whole and hot. A 4 lb Scotch salmon grilse (that is a young fish) is a feast for at least 12 people.

This is simmered (NOT boiled) in a salmon kettle with ½ lb salt and just covered with boiling water. I put the fish in with about ½ pt of water and bring to the boil. Then I pour boiling water in from 6 kettles & finally the salt. Put on a lid & just simmer.

There are many suitable sauces — but as usual I find the simplest the best. ½ lb butter in a jug with juice of 1 lemon. When the butter melts it is ready. This recipe is only suitable for a whole fish.

## FOR A SMALL DINNER PARTY

If catering for a less ambitious number of people allow 4 - 6 oz a head and put the salmon in a well buttered casserole with a cup of white wine, a sprig of fennel and a little salt & ground black pepper.

Bake with the lid on for 40 minutes at No 4.

Dish the fish on to a hot platter. Strain the juice & thicken with beurre manié. Finally stir in a little cream.

## Salmon served cold.

The recipe above for a whole fish may be used. Only simmer for 10 minutes and allow the fish to cool in the liquor (lid on) overnight!

## TROUT.

Most people grill or fry trout.
I prefer them baked.
Well butter a baking dish. Preferably
one pretty enough to go from oven to
table.
Put the trout in and brush generously
with melted butter.
Cover with buttered grease proof paper-
butter side down.
Bake for 20 minutes at No 4.
While they are baking fry flaked
almonds in the rest of the butter.
    Serve with lemon wedges.
Cooked this way the skin is edible.
I think it's the best part ~~

A cream sauce to serve with trout.
From the JURA.    I cup cream.
2 tablespoons chicken stock.  Salt
and pepper.   Add 1 teaspoon of chopped
fennel, one of chives, one of tarragon
and 2 of parsley.  Finally grate a
little lemon zest in.   Warm and
serve.
If a thicker sauce is preferred
make the sauce without the cream.
Whip the cream until thick and
fluffy and fold in at the last minute.

## TURBOT

A whole 6lb Turbot baked will serve 6–8 portions
This is an extravagant dish and must not be
overcooked or the shrinkage is unbelievable.
It is advisable to ask for a cock turbot as
the hen is often full of roe ~ and this is the most
expensive way of buying roe imaginable!

Well butter a baking dish and put in the
turbot ~ black side down. Cut 2 rashers of streaky
bacon into small pieces. Dot the top of the
turbot with dabs of butter and pieces of bacon.
Sprinkle with a very little salt & a lot of
freshly ground black pepper. Cover with a
buttered sheet of grease-proof paper - butter
side down. Bake at No 4 for between 40
minutes & an hour. Slip a fish knife
down to the bone. The minute the flesh comes
away from the bone it is cooked.

Make a sauce from the pan juices.
Add lemon juice, beurre manié and a little
cream. (heat the cream but try not to boil it)

## SEA BASS

A whole fish is very good cooked the same
way as the Salmon on page 95 and served
either hot or cold.

Hot it is good with cucumber sauce (p26)

Grilled it is very good with beurre blanc
recipe (p 31).

# HALIBUT DROPS
sufficient for 4 helpings

1lb of halibut (No skin - no bone)
1 glass sherry. 1 egg. 1oz butter. 1oz cornflour
salt, pepper, crisp breadcrumbs.
Deep oil for frying.

Cook the fish in the sherry, salt & pepper.
2 to three minutes should be time enough.
Mix the butter & flour to-gether & stir in the fish.
When cold, using two dessert spoons to-gether take
out the halibut drops.

Moisten them in the beaten egg & dry them in
the breadcrumbs. Leave for some time before
frying in the hot oil.

30 Seconds in the boiling oil & they are ready
Drain on absorbent paper & serve with lemon.

# FRESH HADDOCK

For 4 portions.   4 portions of haddock filletted
and skinned - the fishmonger
will help with this.

Butter a fire proof dish & put in the haddock.
Melt an oz of butter in a small pan, fry in
1oz flour, add a coffee cup of milk and a teacup
of white wine or cider. Taste & add salt
and pepper.   Pour over the fish.   Lastly
cover the fish with a lot of grated cheese.
Bake at No 4 for about 30 minutes.
If the cheese is not brown enough finish it
off under the grill.

## COQUILLE de MER

Originally this recipe was one of my Mother's. It was a simple dish of equal quantities, after filleting and skinning of fresh haddock, halibut and turbot. For 6 portions 12 oz of fish was barely cooked for about 2 minutes in ½ pt milk and a ¼ pt wine, with salt, pepper and a twist of lemon peel. The subsequent juice was then thickened with an oz of butter and an oz of flour and a good handful of grated cheese. 6 scallops shells (buttered) are then filled and grilled until bubbling and golden brown. This is a very good dish but over the 6 years lobsters, scallops, prawns and conger eel and other exotica have found their way into it. In any form it is delicious ~ especially for dinner party use when it looks so professional.

Mother used to use this mixture for summer picnic sandwiches using wholemeal bread, mayonnaise instead of butter and a few slices of cucumber to add a toothsome crunch to the whole.

~99~

# LOBSTER LOAF

This recipe was given me in 1947 by Col. Ross — one of the first people to realise the potential of frozen food. He said this was his favourite way of eating lobster.

Take a French loaf and split it into two lengthways. Remove the soft white bread. Use chopped up lobster meat and plenty of soft butter. Dust with cayenne pepper and sprinkle in a little lemon juice. Fill the cavity in the loaf and tie together with string in two or three places. Chill in the fridge.

Finally give the loaf ten minutes in the oven at No. 4. and serve cut into door steps.

Extravagant — but really rather special.

## SMOKED HADDOCK with MUSHROOMS

FOR 4 :

| | |
|---|---|
| 4 scallop shells | 8oz smoked haddock after skinning. |
| 4oz mushrooms | 1 small chopped onion |
| 2oz butter | 1oz plain flour. |
| 2oz grated cheese | Salt and pepper. |
| A little milk and white wine or cider. | |

Put the haddock in a basin and cover with boiling water. After about 5 minutes it will be possible to flake the fish and discard any skin and bone.

Melt the butter and simmer the onion for about 10 mins and then fry in the sliced mushrooms for about 1 minute. Stir in the flour and add a little milk to make a really thick sauce. Thin with the wine or cider to the consistency of double cream. Add half the cheese and all the fish. Pour into 4 buttered shells — cover with the rest of the cheese & grill until golden & bubbling.

# CHAPTER SIX
## Roasts & Grills. Meat & Poultry. Dry Frying
### Other dishes using raw meat

---

## Roasted Loin of Veal    3½ hrs slow roasting at No 2.

Get the butcher to chine the loin or it will be impossible to carve. Allow one chop bone at least for a portion.        Stuff the cavity under the loin with

### Parsley stuffing   (for 6 portions).    1 cup fresh brown breadcrumbs.
Enough chopped parsley to turn the mixture green. 4 shallots chopped very fine, a little grated lemon zest, juice of half a lemon, teaspoon of fresh chopped thyme, egg, a lot of butter, salt & pepper. Can be improved by adding 2 rashers chopped streaky bacon and a minced raw chicken liver ~ also a little chopped celery.

Butter the upperside of the loin well and roast. When dishing up do not worry if some stuffing has escaped into the pan juices as this only improves the flavour and thickens the gravy. Dish and make the gravy by adding the other half of the lemon's juice and a little more grated zest. Add vegetable water and stock. If a smooth gravy is preferred pass through a sieve.
A dessertspoon of dryish sherry improves this gravy.

## Roasted Loin of Pork

This can be cooked the same way as the leg (p110). but it does not need a trivet and the stuffing goes underneath. Make sure that the butcher chines it or the carver will be put out !

Allow ½ lb a head and roast for 2 hours at No 3.    First 20 minutes at No 9 to start the crackling off.

# CHATEAUBRIAND

This is fillet steak grilled in a lump.
The Vicomte de Châteaubriand was the French
Ambassador in London in 1822. This famous
dish was given his name by his chef M. Lefort.
Allow 6 oz for a portion and grill fiercely; about
10 minutes each side.   Put on a hot dish and carve
in slices at table.   It should be served with:

## CHATEAUBRIAND SAUCE

Use equal quantities of demi-glace (this is the
natural juice which comes out of joints and poultry when
roasted and which forms a natural jelly) sauce
espagnole or gravy and white wine. Juice $\frac{1}{2}$ lemon
Simmer until reduced by half
and add red currant jelly to
taste. (About a teaspoonful).

Châteaubriand.

# BOEUF WELLINGTON.

This is an excellent dish for entertaining. It can be prepared in the morning and must rest for at least an hour in the fridge.
It takes 35 minutes at No 7 to cook and is just about foolproof.

2 lbs fillet steak makes 4 good helpings. If the Dinner party is for 6, 3 lbs is necessary but the other ingredients will be found to be sufficient.     Pare the fillet of any fat or gristle and fry in a little hot oil for 2 or three minutes on all sides to seal the meat. Set aside to cool.

Now you need ½ lb of pastry. I prefer short-crust but flaky is just as suitable. Make a duxelle of chopped shallot & mushrooms. 12 oz of each cooked in butter (lid on low heat, salt & pepper).     Now scramble 2 eggs in. It goes a horrid grey ~ but fearnot! Take off the heat & allow to cool. Add chopped parsley.

Roll out the pastry into a square the same length and breadth as the fillet.
Put the duxelle in the centre of the pastry. Lay the fillet on diagonally and cover with the rest of the duxelle. Now cover with the pastry like an envelope + moisten the edges so that the pastry seals well. Put into the fridge. Just before cooking brush with egg yolk and milk.

Serve with a rich beef gravy such as Châteaubriand sauce ~ (p. 102).

# HOW TO CARVE A SHOULDER

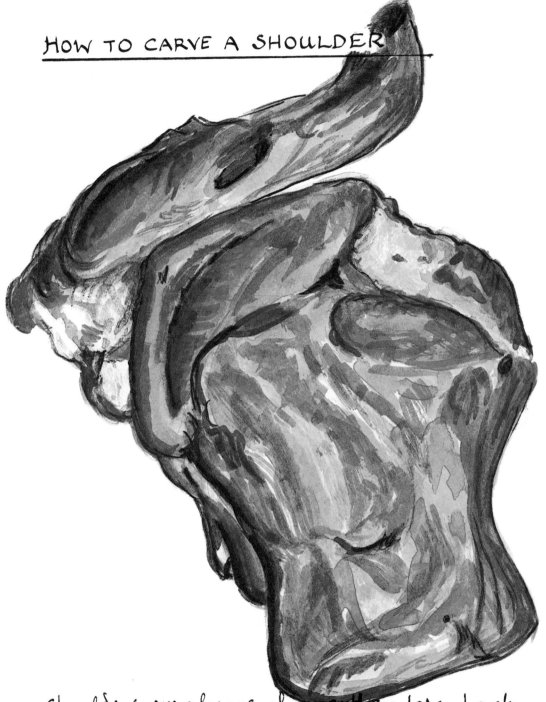

Shoulders are always cheaper than legs. I prefer the meat which is more tender & sweeter. Veal, pork & shoulder bacon can all be carved the same way.

# ROASTED SHOULDER of LAMB

A 3½ lb shoulder of lamb serves 7 portions.

I like to roast turnips underneath. Cut 2lb of turnips into sugar lump sized cubes. Boil them for 5 minutes & keep the water. Cut the knuckle from the shoulder & simmer it in the turnip water to make the gravy.

Put the turnips in a heap on the greased baking tin. Put the shoulder on top of the turnips so that the cavity covers them.

Roast at No 2 for three hours. This may sound a long while but cooked thus the fat melts and the meat is tender and delicious.

Put the joint on a hot dish. Don't penalise the carver by using a small dish. The carver must have plenty of room. Pour off the fat into a dripping basin and sprinkle a little plain flour into the pan juices — the turnip, of course, by this time is in a vegetable dish — pour in the stock & adjust the seasoning with salt & pepper.

Good served with onion sauce, (p. 25) mint sauce (p. 31) and red currant jelly.

To CARVE Lay the shoulder the wrong way up - that is with the crisp skin underneath. Hold the knife horizontally and cut slices flat from all over this side. Then turn over and repeat on the other side. The meat around the shoulder blade comes away easily.

# HOW TO CARVE A SIRLOIN.
## OR A WING RIB
(or any other type of Loin).

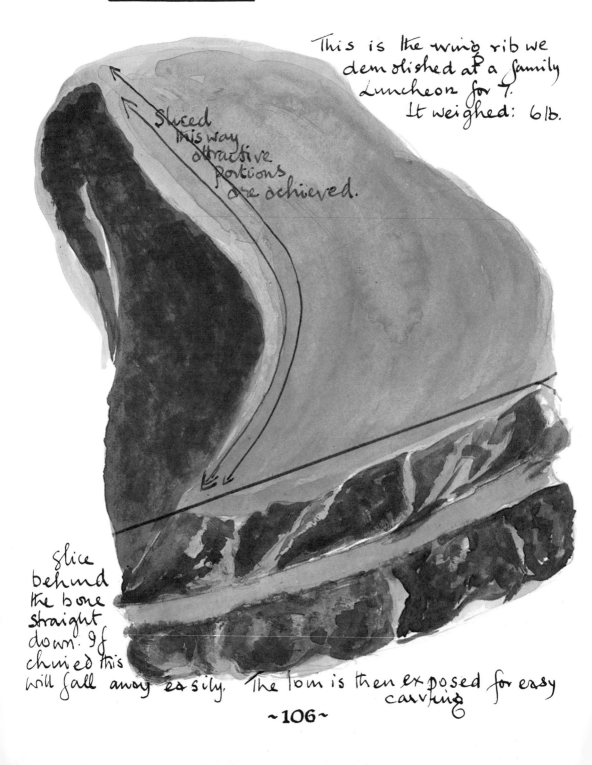

This is the wing rib we
demolished at a family
luncheon for 7.
It weighed: 6lb.

Sliced
this way
attractive
portions
are achieved.

Slice
behind
the bone
straight
down. If
chimed this
will fall away easily. The loin is then exposed for easy
carving

# ROASTED SIRLOIN of BEEF.

For a large family party there is nothing better than a Sirloin. If you remember James the I thought the loin such a noble beast that he knighted it! A wing rib weighing about 5lbs is the next best thing A 15 lb sirloin will just fit into the ordinary domestic cooker. Make sure that the butcher chines it or the carver will be in trouble.

Roast for 2 hrs at No 3. This will give you crisp fat, two or three well done slices either end and a beautiful rare red centre. If you like it better done give it 3 hours. The wing rib will take the same time as girth and not weight determine the cooking time.

A little extra flourish is to pour butter, lemon juice & mustard over the fat as it goes to table. Use a tablespoon as a measure & heat equal quantities of butter, lemon juice & french mustard in a small pan until it seethes. Pour over the fat & sprinkle generously with parsley.

## HORSERADISH CREAM.

About a tablespoon ful of fresh grated horse radish. 1 teaspoon of dry mustard and one of sugar. Mix together with a little malt vinegar and finish by adding about 2 oz of whipped cream and a little salt.

# How to carve a LEG of Pork, Gammon, Lamb, Veal etc
## SUGAR BAKED GAMMON

Place the leg
in this position
and starting at
the narrow end
carve towards you
gradually working
up to the top. This
spreads the fat round
evenly and makes many
attractive slices.

It is very easy to bake a gammon. It is a splendid dish for a private reception and can be served either hot or cold.

A gammon usually weighs between 12-16 lbs. Soak the gammon in cold water for 24 hours. Throw away the water. I hate throwing anything away but this is useless! Place the gammon in a saucepan and cover with cold water adding a lb of brown sugar. I don't know how but this seems to counteract the salt. Bring to the boil and then, with the lid on barely simmer for 2 hours.

When cool enough to handle lift out and skin. I thread the skin on string and hang it up for the tits in my garden. Score the fat slightly until the gammon is divided into diamonds. Put a clove in the centre of each diamond. Pour ½ pt cider and a glass of sherry over the gammon. Make a paste of cider, mustard and brown sugar and brush this on to the fat. Sprinkle a little additional brown sugar on top. Bake for 20 minutes at No 5.

Keep an eye on it as it can burn to a disastrous colour instead of emerging a glorious golden brown.

If to be served hot thicken the pan juices and serve as gravy. If too sweet; sour with a little mustard and malt vinegar.

The gammon opposite (roughly half scale) was 15 lbs 15 oz. One this size should serve about 25 portions.

Roasted leg of Pork. This will serve about 20.
Get the butcher to bone but not roll the leg.
Treat the crackling by scraping savagely with
a sharp knife and rub salt in. Make a sage
and onion stuffing:

2 cups fresh breadcrumbs.
2 large onions chopped coarsely & simmered
in water for 10 minutes.
Salt, pepper & a dessertspoonful fresh chopped
                                              sage,

If you use dried sage use half the quantity.
Mix these ingredients together and stuff the
cavity where the bone was.
Set on a trivet in a baking tin. The wire
from the grill dish does quite well for this.
Brush the crackling with a little olive
oil. Cook at No 9 for 20 minutes to get
the crackling going then reduce to No 3
Total cooking time 3 hours as it is dan-
gerous to serve pork underdone.
Very good served with Sauce Robert (p28)
instead of the traditional apple. (p. 32).
Simmer the bone in the onion water as stock
for the gravy.
      A smaller joint may be cooked the same
way and will take approximately the same time
in the oven because the cooking is influenced
by the girth and not the weight. If the joint
weighs less than 3lbs cook it at No 2.

      The shoulder is cheaper and I think
a better buy.

~110~

# CAPON ROASTED IN WHITE WINE

This recipe needs a good farm chicken. A 6lb capon serves 8. The trick is to find a saucepan which really fits the bird with a good lid

Melt 4oz butter and fry 1 bayleaf, parsley and thyme. Now seal the bird turning frequently in this mixture. It makes a fantastic aroma~ Now pour in ½ pint white wine ~ put on the lid & simmer for an hour.

When cool enough to handle take out ~ be careful not to scald yourself with the very hot liquid in the inside of the bird. Brush the bird with salted beaten egg and cover with breadcrumbs~ the crisp ones. You will find nothing sticks very well. Allow to dry and try again ~ more egg & more crumbs. This time you will find it sticks. Cover thoroughly and put in a buttered roasting tin. Roast at No 4 for an hour. It should come out crisp & golden. To make the sauce strain the juice in the sauce pan and simmer to reduce. Very good flavoured with marigold petals and egg yolks. or cream.

~111~

Bramleys

## Roasted Pheasant

One pheasant serves four.
Well butter the roasting tin.
Butter a slice of brown bread and cover with pâté.*
Place this in the tin with the pheasant on top.
Brush with melted butter and cover with streaky
  bacon.    Roast for 50 minutes at No 7.
Dish the pheasant.   Make the gravy the usual
way with the addition of a glass of port.
*If you butter the bread both sides it stops it sticking.

Serve with breadcrumbs fried in butter.
Red currant jelly, game chips and watercress.


## Dry-fried Steak.    unless you have a silver
grill heated by charcoal the best way to grill
a steak is to dry fry it.    You need a very old
frypan that never sticks.  A non-stick is no
good.    Grease the pan with a butter paper.
Get the pan really hot & then hold the
steak down on this heat for a minute. Turn
and repeat.  Now reduce the heat and cook
until ready - rare 4 minutes, medium 6.
A well done steak is not satisfactory cooked
                                          this way

# ROASTED GUINEA FOWL

A plump guinea fowl serves 3 or even 4 portions. It can be cooked just the same as a pheasant (p 112). We are fortunate in having a local farmer who grows them up to 3¾ lbs.

Here is a recipe using watercress stuffing and sauce. It is one of Rosalind's:

1 guinea fowl.

For the stuffing: 1 chopped onion softened in butter
1 Bundle of watercress, chopped (stems & all).
1 cup of brown bread crumbs. 1 oz butter.

Mix to a soft stuffing ~ if dry add more butter. Season with salt and pepper. The beauty of making stuffing is that if it tastes good raw it will taste even better cooked. This makes it easy to get the seasoning right.

Stuff the bird loosely. Brush with melted butter. Roast at No 6. for an hour ~ the stuffing makes the longer time and lower heat necessary.

The sauce is made like gravy. Cook a chopped onion in butter until tender. Dish the bird and sprinkle flour into the tin ~ fry and add some good stock or milk. Add the onion with its butter, a tablespoonful of chopped watercress, salt and pepper and bring to the boil. Add a little cream and serve ~ If you don't like "bits" either sieve or liquidize

## GUINEA FOWL (An Italian recipe.)

Season a guinea fowl with salt. pepper and minced juniper berries. (about 10). Fry all over in butter and put in a casserole with 2 tablespoons of stock and 1 tablespoon brandy. Cover and cook for 40 minutes at No 4. While this is cooking soak a handful of white grapes ~ seeded (or seedless ones) and roughly chopped in a coffee cup of white wine and 1 tablespoon brandy.

Take the lid off the bird and add the grapes, their juice, and a tablespoon of marsala. Cook for 15 more minutes with the lid off. Place the bird on a serving dish and thicken the pan juices with chestnut purée and serve as gravy.

## CHICKEN ROASTED in Marsala. (a Sicilian recipe.)

For 4. A 4lb chicken. ¼lb butter, A small tin of peeled tomatoes, or 4 peeled fresh ones. ¼pt Marsala. About 2oz grated cheese.

Melt the butter, fry in the tomatoes and their juice. Salt and pepper to taste. Butter a roasting tin and put in the chicken. Pour over the butter, tomato, marsala mixture. Roast for 1 hour at No 5 basting with the pan juices 3 times. Now cover the breast with the grated cheese and return to the oven until the breast is the colour of ripe wheat. Serve with rice and use the pan juices just as they are as sauce. Good with spinach. The original recipe adds a pint of mussels to the rice at the last moment before serving.

# ROASTED DUCKLING with apples & cider

A 4lb duckling. Smaller ones are only skin & grief.

1 small bottle dry cider.      4oz double cream.

For the stuffing

3 oz butter. 4oz white breadcrumbs
1lb bramleys cooked to a purée
Salt, pepper, sugar & cinnamon.

Fry the fresh breadcrumbs in the butter until golden brown and crisp. Mix with the apple purée. Taste & season with salt, pepper, sugar & cinnamon. Stuff the duck loosely and roast for 1½ hours at No 3.

Lift the duck into a dry greased pan, pour over the cider and roast for another half hour. Dish. Reduce the cider by rapid boiling and thicken with the cream. Add a little salt & pepper and serve as gravy.

If you set the discarded fat in a deep bowl, next day an amount of duck jelly will have formed at the bottom. This is beautiful for making châteaubriand sauce (p.102). The fat may be used in Terrine of giblets (p.139).

## BASTING

Very rarely do I suggest basting a roast as with thermostatically controlled ovens the amount of heat lost in opening the door cannot compensate for any good it may do.

# HOW TO CARVE A DUCK OR GOOSE

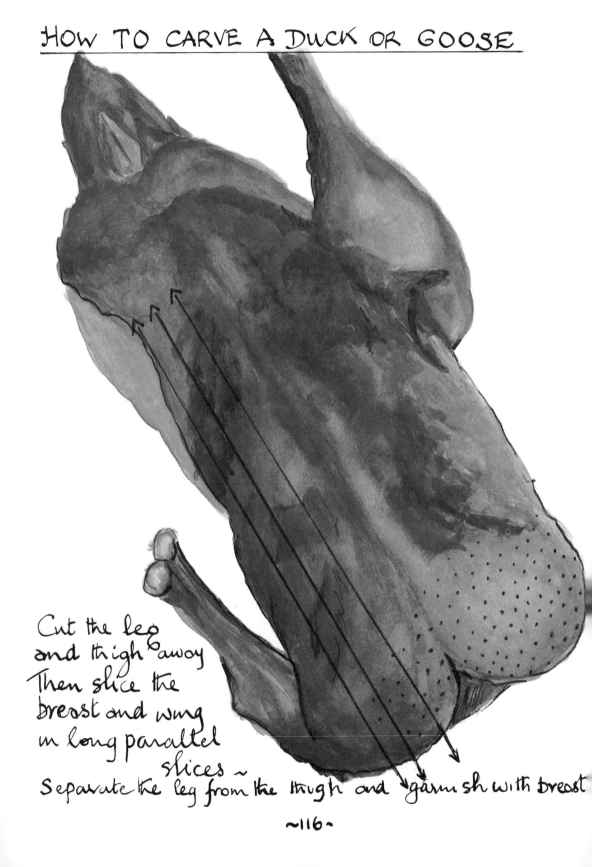

Cut the leg
and thigh away
Then slice the
breast and wing
in long parallel
slices ~
Separate the leg from the thigh and garnish with breast

# ROASTED GOOSE

The traditional way to cook a goose is
to stuff it with sage & onion (p 110) and
serve with apple sauce.

Fill the goose with the stuffing and roast
on a trivet for 3 hours at No 3.
A good goose serves about 8 helpings.

An alternative stuffing is:

Apricot & Almond stuffing

½ lb fresh apricots ~ or dried.
1½ oz flaked almonds. salt & pepper.
1 hand ful of sultanas. 1 lemon ~ rind grated & juice.
Parsley ~ about a chopped table spoonful.

A large onion chopped & softened in butter.
use plenty of butter to cook the onion as it improves
the stuffing. If using dried apricots soak ½ lb
over night and simmer in a very little water. If
fresh just cut away from the stones & break the stones
with a hammer & use the kernels.

Mix all the ingredients to-gether. If too moist
add a very few fresh breadcrumbs ~ if too dry add
a little apricot juice or white wine.

## Apple, Celery & Walnut Stuffing.

2 onions, chopped & softened in 2 oz butter. 1 cup fresh
white breadcrumbs. 4 sticks of celery chopped, 1 large
bramley, peeled & sliced. 4 oz walnuts broken up. A lot
of parsley ~ a sprig of thyme, 2 or 3 sage leaves and a sprig
of marjoram. (The herbs all chopped). Dried will do. use less.

Mix the ingredients together adding enough cream
to moisten the stuffing. Equally suitable for pork
duck or goose ~

# HOW TO CARVE A CHICKEN, TURKEY OR PHEASANT

wishbone

Turn the bird on it's side and take off the leg, thigh. Separate these and then carve away from the exposed breast. Repeat other side.

# ROASTED FARMYARD CHICKEN

A good farm bird ~ preferably a capon.
A 6lb bird will serve 8 helpings.

Take the fat out of the inside ~ a good farm
bird always has a nice lump inside ~ chop
roughly (scissors are best) and mix it with
the stuffing. It is difficult to improve on
the veal stuffing (page 101).

Stuff the bird taking care to leave it
loosely inside. If packed firm it cannot
gather up and retain the lovely juices
that flow into it while it is roasting.
Brush the bird with melted butter and
roast for 2 hours at No 3.

While the bird is roasting summer
the neck & gizzard with the wing tips ~ which
are better off ~ an onion, a carrot, a stick
of celery & a bouquet garni. This will make
a good strong stock for the gravy. The liver
and heart will be in the stuffing.

If you have some stuffing over form
it into little false meat balls & put them
in the baking dish for the last half hour.

Dish the bird onto a hot platter ~ a
large one so that the carver is not handicapped.
Pour off the surplus fat. Sprinkle the pan with
a little plain flour, brown. Add the stock.
Salt & pepper to taste and a little red wine.

To carve the breast use the angle of the
wishbone as a guide line.

## CHICKEN: LEGS & THIGHS with COURGETTES

For 4 portions:

4 chicken legs & thighs cut into 8 pieces
Melt the 2oz of butter in on oven proof dish.
Put in the legs & thighs and sprinkle with salt
& freshly milled pepper. Pour over the butter.
Brush the chicken joints with the melted butter
around them ~ cover them with chopped parsley
(about a tablespoonful) and sprinkle with the
juice of the lemon.

Cook for an hour at No 4.

Take a lb of courgettes and cut in thick
rings (about ½" thick) Simmer for 2 or 3
minutes after they come to a boil. Drain well.
When the chicken has cooked for 20 minutes
introduce the courgette around and beneath
the chicken. Brush them with the melted
butter mixture in the dish.

Baste every 20 minutes.
Serve with rice using the pan juices as sauce.

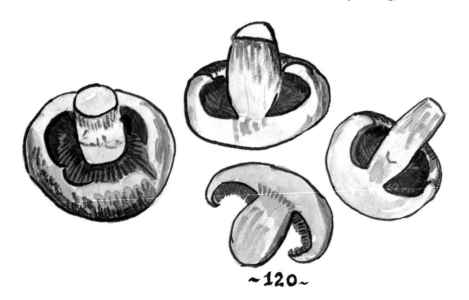

# Escalop of Veal with Cream

For 6 portions.    Six escalop of veal beaten flat.
1 cup double cream,   1 cup of Marsala or dry Vermouth
2 oz seasoned flour (p. 10).
Ask your butcher to prepare the escalops.
Pour the Marsala or Vermouth into a soup plate.
Melt 2 oz butter in a largish pan that is good
tempered and does not stick.

Dip the escalop in the wine and then dry both
sides in the flour. Fry in the butter ~ about 3 mins
each side.    Pour in the cream and Summer for
2 or three minutes.    Serve with slices of lemon
If any wine is left mix it with the rest of the
seasoned flour and add to the sauce before
introducing the cream.

I like this dish sprinkled with rosemary.
If the sauce is too thick, thin with a little white
stock. Leg of pork can be cooked the same way.

## CARRE D'AGNEAU ~ RACK OF LAMB (John's recipe)

Trim a rack of all fat, except to leave a thin
amount at the top to protect the meat.
Roast in a very hot oven No 8 for 15-20
minutes. This is a French way of cooking
lamb. 1 rack does 3 good helpings. The
lamb is very tender and underdone. It is
not a suitable dish for those who like well
cooked meat. Garlic may be slipped between meat & bone.
Good served with mint butter (p. 34).
and new potatoes.
This joint cooks best using a trivet in the
baking tin. (p. 110).

## CANETON à l'ORANGE (Larry's recipe).

1 duckling (a 4lb one if possible). 1 orange.

Peel off the outer rind finely in long strips from top to bottom of the orange. Finally cut the strips into very fine Julienne strips. Squeeze out the orange juice and reserve. Pooch the rind for a few minutes in boiling water. Throw away the water and replace with cold water.

Season the duck with salt and pepper and put the remains of the orange ~ pulp and pith ~ inside the carcass. Roast on a trivet for 1 hr at No 6 Now pat the duck with kitchen paper to remove excess fat and to get a really crisp skin. Return to the oven. and give the duck another 30 minutes at No. 7

Dish the duck and leave in a minimum heat in the oven. Carefully pour off the fat from the roasting tray leaving the natural juices. Reduce these with rapid boiling to a small amount of caramel liquid. Sprinkle with a little flour, stir well and add the orange juice. Strain into a sauce boat and add the orange peel (drained).

# TOURNEDOS FLAMBE

1 tot brandy. 4 tournedos Garlic. 1oz melted butter.
4 strips red pimento. 4 rounds of fried bread    Put the
garlic through a press and add to the butter. Paint the tournedos
with this. When set turn over and brush the other side. Fry the
bread & put on a dish in the oven. Fry the steaks in a dry pan —
about 2 minutes each side. Pour in brandy and set alight.
Set one steak on a round of bread & garnish with pimento.

# SHOULDER of LAMB à la Gasconne

Get the butcher to bone a shoulder — but not
to roll it. Start the bones off in a small stockpot
with an onion etc ready for the gravy.
The difference in this dish is the exciting
stuffing.

1 Cup of soft white breadcrumbs.
½ lb minced ham or bacon.
1 small onion chopped. Garlic if liked.
1 egg.
Salt and freshly milled black pepper.
½ cup of flaked almonds.
12 juniper berries.
1 dessert spoon fresh chopped tarragon.
¼ pt of duck fat (or butter). (use half if dried)
Rosemary, mint and parsley — a teaspoon of each.

Mix the stuffing well and fill the bone cavity.
Finish off by securing with skewers — or needle
and thread.
Roast for 2½ hrs at No. 3.

## ANOTHER WAY WITH FILLET.

4 small fillet steaks. Beat them between greaseproof paper until twice their size.

Seethe together 1 tablespoon of butter, 1 tablespoon of French mustard and 1 tablespoon of lemon juice. Fry the steaks in this ~ 1½ minutes each side. Serve on fried bread, cover with the pan juices and sprinkle with chopped parsley.

An alternative flavour ~ use tarragon instead of parsley.

This is a good dish to serve with the first new potatoes and a mixed watercress and lettuce salad.

## PORK FILLET with Mushrooms.

For 4 large or 6 normal portions:
A 2lb Pork fillet. If this is unobtainable the fat trimmed meat of the loin can be used. Cut into 4 or 6 rounds and beat out with a mallet ~ or a rolling pin. Dry in seasoned flour (p.10) and fry in butter ~ about 2 minutes each side. Put into a low oven while preparing the other ingredients. Fry 4 or 6 rounds of crustless bread and then 2 mushrooms for each portion. Dish the meat onto the bread and place the mushrooms on top. Fry a little flour in the pan and pour in ½ cup white wine and ½ cup of cream. Taste, season and pour over.

# CHAPTER SEVEN
## Puddings

It is difficult to cook well if you do not like the end product! I am not fond of sugar and sweet things. One of my friends once said: "Joan's puds are awful – but at least they are alcoholic!"

Anyway here are just a few recipes which I have found very useful and acceptable – the first being a foolproof way of making Victoria Sponges

# VICTORIA SPONGE

2 eggs. their weight in butter, vanilla sugar and self raising flour.

Melt the butter but be careful <u>not</u> to overheat. Separate whites from yolks. Beat whites stiff. Beat in the caster sugar, then the yolks and finally the butter. Sift the flour into the mixture and stir in very gently with a spoon.

Butter two 7" or 8" sponge tins.

Pour half the mixture into each. With a knife draw the mixture to the edges leaving the centre lower. Pre heat the oven at No 5 and cook for about 15 minutes. If a skewer comes out clean the sponges are cooked. Leave to cool & shrink for a few minutes. Then turn out onto a wire to cool.

With these sponges here are two good White
Russian recipes:

## COFFEE GATEAU.

Prick a sponge all over with a Knitting needle.
Then soak with ½ pt of doubly strong instant
coffee. This takes a long time, I pour some more
on everytime I pass ~ (only if stale ~ a fresh one gets too wet
and needs draining).

Now ice with butter icing. 2 ozs soft butter 3 oz Icing sugar.
Cream together and then add two or three teaspoons
of coffee ~ just enough to make it possible to pour the
Icing over. (Care ful ~ it needs very little coffee).

Set to cool in the fridge.

When the icing is fairly firm smother in
whipped cream & sprinkle flaked almonds*
generously all over. *These may be toasted in the oven.

## RASPBERRY & REDCURRANT GATEAU

This can only be made in the summer when
both fresh raspberries & fresh red currants
are available.

1 lb redcurrants put in ¾ pt water & boiled.
NO sugar. Strain & Keep the juice.

Soak the sponge with this juice.

Make Butter icing as in the coffee gâteau and
thin with a very little red currant juice.

Pour the icing over & set in the fridge.

Finally cover generously with whipped
cream and cover with rings of fresh raspberries.

## Rum & Apricot Gâteau (one of mine!)

This needs two sponges.
1lb fresh apricot cooked with very little sugar.
Soak the lower sponge in apricot juice.
Cover with Apricot jam.
Cover with the other sponge (dry).
Cover with the Apricot halves. Break
the stones open & sprinkle the Kernels over.
  Make a syrup of the rest of the apricot water
demerara sugar, butter & rum. Roughly
equal quantities but only one tot of Navy rum.
Pour this over the top and decorate the sides
with whipped cream.
  Don't worry if you don't like rum. It tastes
entirely different in puddings.


## CHESTNUT PUDDING.

Chestnuts mashed with sugar and butter.
Tinned will do but they are too wet. Dried
can be soaked overnight & simmered until
tender. A much better flavour.
  Cream beaten with vanilla sugar and as much
olososo (cream) sherry as it will take ~ added
teaspoon by teaspoon.

  Put alternate layers in a cut glass bowl
ending with a layer of cream. Decorate the
top with tangerine segments.

 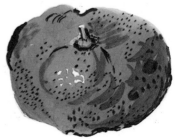

## PAVLOVA   (An Australian friend's recipe)

Pre-heat the oven at No 3.

Take 4 or 5 egg whites (depending on the size)
1 teacup granulated sugar. (Vanilla pods can be kept in
grad. too).
Beat whites stiff and then gradually beat in the
sugar.          Now beat in 1 teaspoonful of
vinegar and 2 teaspoonsfuls of corn flour.

Wet a piece of greaseproof paper on both sides.
Place on a flat baking tin.    Run the papered
tin under the tap so that it is sopping wet.
Now pile on the pavlova in a flattened heap.

Put into the oven and reduce the heat to No 1.
Leave for an hour.  Finally place upside down
on a serving dish and pull off the greaseproof.

When cool fill with whipped cream and passion
fruit pips.    Very good with unsweetened
raspberries or blackcurrants.

## MERINGUES

Are very easy to make, yet, so often, seem to have a sort of bogey about them.

After making them for years without any trouble one day they flopped. The only difference I could think of was the baking tin. We'd lent the thick sheets to the Girl Guides for their fête. So half the secret of success is to us a very thick baking tin. Butter it well. All you have to remember is that one white of egg needs two ounces of castor sugar. Eggs are best at room temperature.

Whip the whites stiff ~ gradually add the sugar. Pipe or spoon the meringue on to the buttered tin and cook at the lowest heat ~ NOT at a quarter but as low as the regulo tap can be turned back.

Cook for about 1½ hrs. If the meringues stick to the buttered tray put them somewhere hot for a few seconds ~ just to unfreeze the butter.

If a few drops of vinegar are added to the mixture the result is a marsh mallow instead of a meringue.

## PALOBO

This is a sticky Spanish chocolate mousse ~ very morish ~

6 eggs. 4 oz milk chocolate. 8 oz bitter chocolate. 6 oz sugar. 6 ozs butter.

Separate the whites & yolks. Beat yolks and sugar together until light and fluffy. Whisk in melted chocolate & butter. (The chocolate and butter soon melt in a bain marie.) Lastly with a clean dry whisk, whisk the whites really stiff and fold into the mixture.  Pour into a pretty bowl and leave to set in the fridge.

## SHORT CRUST PASTRY

This is my foolproof method that is as useful as the Victoria sponge recipe.  Remember with pastry that the less you handle it the better it will taste.

8 oz Self raising flour.
2 oz butter.
2 oz Vegetable fat (Spry, Cookeen or Trex).
1 teaspoon salt,
A squeeze of lemon juice.
Iced water (about ½ a cupful).

Sift the flour into a mixing bowl. Take the butter and fat from the fridge so that it is hard and grate on an ordinary grater into the flour.  If it feels sticky roll it in the flour as you go along.  Sprinkle in the salt. Now mix using only the very tips of the fingers and keep moving the fat and the flour up to gather up air.  Rub together until the mixture looks like fine breadcrumbs. Rinse & dry the fingers. Add the lemon juice and most of the iced water it is easy to add more but difficult to subtract. Mix with a knife until a dough forms.  Knead very lightly for a few seconds. Flour a board and roll out.

# RUM SOUFFLE OMELETTE

As a hopeless pudding cook this is my one big moment ~ the really show-off dessert! You need to be organised and then it's easy.

Allow 1 egg for each portion. I find about 4 portions ~ 6 at a push ~ the most you can manage successfully ~ but you do need a large frying pan of the old-fashioned non-stick variety. I don't like the modern ones. They seem to alter the texture and flavour of food.

Separate the whites from the yolks and make sure the whites are in a bowl large enough for them to be whipped.

Now make the sauce in a small saucepan. For 4 people I use the kitchen double tablespoon. One full of butter, one full of demerara and one of rum. (This of course is level & half the amount of the other ingredients.) Melt together, bring to the boil and cook for 2 or 3 minutes. I find the Navy type rum is for me the best flavour in cooking.

Next melt about 2oz butter into the frying pan. Stand over it and roll it round so that it sets evenly when left to cool.

Having made these preparations the soufflé can be produced in about 2 minutes. The getting ready part can be seen to hours before. Get your husband or someone to clear the table slowly and to chat amusingly (!) and go and do your bit of conjuring. 4 hot plates at the ready; start to warm the buttered frying pan and whip the whites stiff. Eye on the pan as the butter must not brown. Whip the yolks into the whites. Now put the sauce on to warm and get all the fluffy egg into the frying pan. Increase the heat under this and watch until minute little bubbles of air start to appear above the fluff. This means that the omlette is ready. Flip it over so that it doubles into a half moon. Stir the sauce and pour it all over the top. Pick up the four hot plates in one hand and the frying pan in the other and return to the dining room. Cut it into four and serve. I shall be surprised if you don't like it! A practice run "à deux" before showing off might be a good idea ~~~

## RUM & CHOCOLATE SHAPE

1 pint milk
2 oz butter
2 oz demerara
6 oz bitter chocolate (or plain ~ milk is too mild)
1 Tablespoon rum.
2 oz cornflour.

In a 2 pt basin mix the cornflour and just enough of the milk to smooth it into a thick mixture (rather like quick-sand)

Melt the chocolate, demerara & rum in a double saucepan with the butter.

Boil the milk and pour foaming onto the cornflour mixture & stir well. Add the melted chocolate mixture*

Wet a mould. Pour in the shape and leave overnight to set.

Turn out and serve with whipped cream.      Wolf used to love this pud.
*If it has not thickened properly bring to the boil without boiling stirring constantly.

# FLAMED PEACHES

6 ripe peaches. ½ pt water.
6 oz castor sugar. 4 tablespoons brandy.

Wipe the peaches. Place them in a largish basin. Cover with boiling water & leave for 2 minutes. Lift out and peel. Cut the peaches in half. Remove the stones. Bash these with a hammer to extract the kernels. Blanch to skin & chop the kernels.

Make a syrup of the ½ pt water & castor sugar and boil for two or three minutes. Now add the peaches & their chopped kernels and simmer very gently for 5 minutes. Lift out carefully and arrange in a pretty dish. (should be fireproof)

Reduce the syrup by half by rapid boiling. Strain over the peaches & leave to cool.

Just before serving warm the brandy in a small saucepan. Set it alight, pour over the peaches & serve at once.

# TARTE BOURGEOISE

This is my Belgian grandmother's Apple Tart. For me the perfect follow up to Sunday Roast Beef.

You need the short crust pastry on page 130. This should be sufficient to line an ordinary swiss roll tin. Butter this generously and then see how thin you can roll out the pastry. It doesn't matter if there is the odd hole as this can easily be patched. Just moisten the edges of the patch with a little water so that it sticks.

Now peel and slice Bramley apples – rather thick slices – if they are sliced too thinly there is not enough juice. Arrange the slices in neat overlapping rows. Cover generously with demerara sugar – but be careful to keep it half an inch away from the edges. Cook in a hot oven No 7 (pre-heated) for 35 minutes. After this peep every two or three minutes until the tops of the apples are a rich caramel colour.

Good with or without whipped cream.

The complete tart on the night took 6 Bramleys. There were 6 rows of apple.

Bramleys sliced ready for the tart.

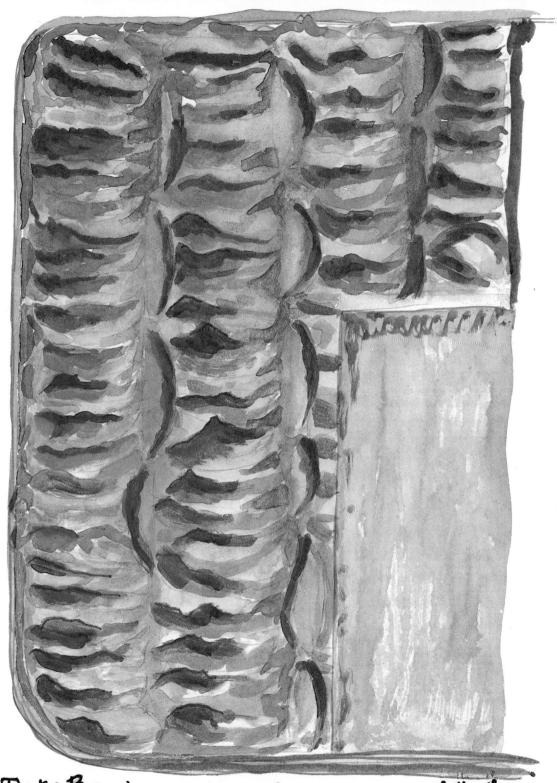

Tarte Bourgeoise (Actual Size) What was left after
Luncheon
-135-

# EVE PUDDING

I learnt this one in a Girl Guide camp in the 30's. But it makes it none the less delicious!

Butter a 2lb pudding basin and half fill with slices of Bramley apples. Push down well & then cover ~ and I mean cover ~ them with about ½" of demerara sugar.   Make the Victoria Sponge mixture on p.125. and pour this in smoothing it off on top.   Cover with two layers of greaseproof paper ~ butter the one nearest the pudding and steam for 2 hours. The basin should be ¾ full.

To steam find a saucepan a little larger than the basin with a good lid.   Put in a trivet and some of the peel of the apples ~ this stops an aluminium saucepan turning black.   The trivet supplied with pressure cookers is excellent for this use. I don't know if you can buy one without the pressure cooker?

Rhubarb is equally good treated this way and has a similar effect on the saucepan ~ not the leaves ~ but the rough bits you usually discard.

# PEARS COOKED IN WINE

6 almost ripe dessert pears.
Peel whole leaving the stalks.
   Make about a pint of syrup using half red wine, half water and 8 oz of gran. sugar. Flavour with 1 stick of cinnamon and a strip of lemon.
   Pour over the pears and either leave covered in a low oven or summer in a closed sauce pan on top of the cooker.
   When the pears are tender remove them to a serving dish and thicken the syrup with a little arrowroot or potato flour. Pour over the pears.
   This dessert is better served cold.

# GINGER MOUSSE

3 eggs,   3 oz Castor Sugar,
5 tablespoons ginger syrup and 3 pieces of stem ginger.
I dessertspoon powdered gelatine softened in 1 tablespoon
of water.  2 tablespoons of boiling water.

Whip the whites stiff.   In another bowl
whip the yolks and sugar together until light and
creamy.   Liquidize the stem ginger in the
syrup.   Add the hot water to the softened gelatine
and stir until dissolved.   Now mix all the
ingredients to-gether folding the whites in last.
Pour into six glass dishes & chill to set.
Serve with whipped cream.


# SHORTBREAD TARTS.

Make the recipe for shortbread on page 79
and then add 2 tablespoons of cold water and
treat like pastry.   Roll out thin and cut with
a circular cutter and bake the empty tarts
in tart trays.   Because the flour is not self-
raising the tarts bake "blind" without any
bother.   These tarts can be filled with many
things.   I like to put in whipped cream and
one or two strawberries or some raspberries.
They are delicious filled with lemon curd.(p78)

# CHAPTER EIGHT
## Savouries, Pâtés & Entrées

### TERRINE of GIBLETS

Rashers of streaky bacon.

4lbs necks, gizzards & hearts
1lb of Veal or Pork.
½lb poultry livers.
1 onion (chopped)
2oz butter. 2 large mushrooms
1 soup ladle of strong stock
5 sprigs tarragon. 3 sorrel leaves

2nd list of ingredients
1 tot brandy (or sherry).
1 teaspoon allspice
Salt, pepper.
1 tablespoon chopped herbs: (parsley, thyme, chives & marjoram).
3oz butter 8 small mushrooms.
1 heaped tablespoon aspic.

Fry onion and butter till softened. Add the stock and two large mushrooms. Put in the necks, hearts, gizzards and veal or pork. Cover closely and simmer for 2 hours with the sprigs of tarragon and the sorrel. Grill the bacon. Butter 2 terrine moulds or bread tins. Cut the bacon into pieces and arrange in the bottom of the moulds. Fry the livers lightly in the bacon fat. When the necks & gizzards are cool enough to handle put 8 gizzards aside and pull as much meat as possible from the necks. Mince all the meat and livers until very smooth. Add the brandy, butter and aspic, allspice and chopped herbs. Taste and add salt and pepper. Put a layer of this mixture into each mould. Slice the button mushrooms and gizzards and arrange through the centre of the moulds. Cover with the rest of the mixture. Cover with foil and bake for an hour at No 4 in a baking tin with water in. Put a weight on top of each mould and leave to cool at least overnight, preferably for 2 days. Unmould and serve in slices.

# KIDNEYS COOKED in RED WINE

This dish is good as an entrée before fish; tasty as a supper snack on toast or served on a small piece of fried bread at the end of Dinner.

2 Pig's Kidneys (If you prefer lamb's you'll need 4)
2 slices bacon, 1 back, 1 streaky.
1 very small onion chopped fine
3 button mushrooms, sliced
1 teaspoon chopped parsley & 2 or 3 sage leaves
A sherry glass of red wine.*    or a pinch of dried.
1 dessertspoon flour, salt & pepper.    * ABOUT 5 floz
2 oz butter.

Wash the Kidneys ~ slip off their thin covering skin, slice thinly and discard the middle tough little bit.    Dry the slices in the flour. Melt butter & cook onion a little (about 8 minutes) next the mushrooms with the onion, and then the Kidneys cooking very slowly and turning frequently. Fast cooking makes offal tough. Sprinkle with salt, pepper and the herbs. Pour in the red wine. Bring to the boil stirring constantly. Cover, reduce the heat, and simmer for about five minutes. Chop the bacon, fry & add.
These quantities sufficient for 4 portions if served as an entrée.
It tastes best if served with hot buttered toast. If any is left over it can be liquidized and thinned with strong meat stock and makes an excellent Kidney soup.    On a cold winter's night with sizzling hot croutons it is very warming. Good for November the Fifth!

~ 140 ~

## MONICA'S EGGS.

This is soft boiled eggs peeled and served in a sweet pepper sauce.      For 4 portions

1 oz butter. ½ oz plain flour.
A small tin of red peppers (chopped) and all their juice
1 hand ful grated cheese.
A little milk.
Salt and freshly milled black pepper.

Make the sauce by frying the butter & flour together, Add the juice from the pimientoes and the chopped pimientoes. Stir and add enough milk to make a sauce of cream like consistency. Add the cheese & stir until it melts. Taste & season with salt and pepper.

Boil the eggs for 4 minutes. Peel & cover with the sauce. Garnish with watercress.

## MADRAS TOASTIE

This is a tasty dish ~ by-product of a well made curry.
You need hot buttered toast.
Left over curry.
Banana & tomato rinds
Dessicated or (far better) freshly grated coconut
Chutney.

Spread the curry generously on the buttered toast & grill till hot. Sprinkle with coconut, decorate with banana & tomato & top with a teaspoon of chutney.

# SHELLFISH RISOTTO

For 4.    8 oz shellfish (Lobster, Scampi, Scallops, Prawns)
or a mixture.
1 onion chopped and cooked in 2 tablespoons of olive
oil, in a chafing dish that will sit on the stove, in the oven
or under the grill and then look good enough to send to
the dining room.

4 heaped table spoons of long grain rice.
4 tablespoons of butter.   1 pt of poultry stock.
Nutmeg, turmeric.
Juice of ½ lemon, 2 tablespoons cream, 1 tablespoon of
golden Syrup.    Grated cheese.   Tinned red peppers
for décor.

If the fish is already cooked chop roughly and add at
the last minute when the pimentoes are used to decorate
the dish.   If raw cut into cubes and introduce at the
same time as the rice.

Add the dry rice to the onion and oil and fry for
a few seconds.   Pour in the boiling stock and add salt
and pepper. Cover and simmer until the rice is tender
(about 12 – 15 minutes)  Take off the lid and stir until
surplus liquid has gone.  Add the butter and
nutmeg for flavour and turmeric mostly for colour – (about
a teaspoon of each).   Put the lemon juice, cream and syrup
in a little saucepan and stir until fluid.

Pour over the top of the risotto. Decorate with strips
of pimiento. Cover generously with grated cheese and
finish in the oven (No4) or under the grill. The dish
should be golden brown and bubbling.

## Smoked Herring

This is always a winner!

It is Kipper fillets sliced off their thick skins and left for two or three hours in lemon juice.

Serve as if smoked salmon with brown bread & butter, lemon wedges & cayenne pepper.

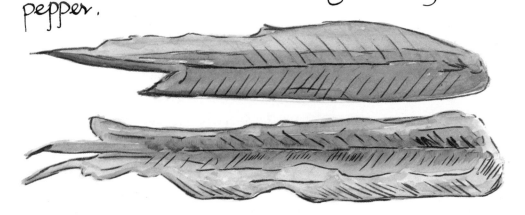

## OMELETTE CARMEN

This is an ordinary French omelette with an interesting filling and sauce. It makes a good entrée.

For 4 portions make a 6 egg omelette. fill with the savoury mixture ~ fold over & cover with sauce. This is far quicker than making 4 omelettes:

Filling 1 Pimiento chopped. 6 oz lobster meat or scampi. 12 Black olives (stoned) Olive oil, garlic, & a chopped onion. Soften the onion & garlic in the oil, add the other ingredients, season & simmer until tender.

Sauce Olive oil. garlic and another chopped onion. Simmer until tender with 6 peeled tomatoes. Season with salt, pepper & mace. Sieve and serve.

## QUICHE LORRAINE

The origin of this dish was for an easy supper dish on bread baking day and the last piece of dough was used to line a circular buttered tin and baked with the egg, bacon, & cream filling.    Short crust pastry (p130) is a good substitute.

For 6 portions take a 9" baking tin, butter and line with pastry.    You will need:
6 rashers of bacon, 2 eggs. ½ pt cream salt, & freshly ground black pepper.

Grill the rashers of bacon until half cooked. When cool enough to handle cut quite small and arrange in the tin. Beat the egg, stir in the cream, salt & pepper & pour into the quiche.    Bake for about 30 minutes at No 6.

## ASPARAGUS QUICHE

This is made the same way using tinned asparagus. Drain the asparagus & keep the water. Cut Asparagus into short lengths and arrange in the quiche. Beat 2 eggs and add ¼ pt cream. Add ¼ pt asparagus water. Season with salt and pepper and bake.

# CHAPTER NINE
## Entertaining

I really enjoy entertaining at home. It is a great pleasure to share a meal with friends. The secret is to keep it simple. Over elaboration only embarrasses your guests and success is achieved when you can sit down calmly and enjoy your own party.

First: choose your menu. Either serve hot, cold, hot courses ~ three are more than enough ~ or cold, hot, cold.

Here are some suggested menus that really work. All the recipes can be found in this book. The quantities are sufficient for 6.

## SPRING

It is a good plan to write out a really detailed menu ~ for your own use, not for the guests. It makes it so much easier not to forget some silly little thing and also to help remember what to buy at the shops. Details of the smoked herring are on p. 143. Two fillets each will be more than ample. Cayenne pepper although the same colour as paprika is entirely different. A lot of grocers fail to realise this ~ ~

# A Spring LUNCHEON

Smoked Herring ~ served
with brown bread & butter
Lemon wedges &
cayenne pepper.

Escolop de Veau à la crème
Ragout de légumes.
Potatoes Anna
Mixed Green Salad.
French Dressing

Ginger Mousse.
Fresh fruit salad.

Cheese Board
Biscuits & Crisp French
Bread

Coffee

# A SPRING DINNER

Pâté maison served with
hot buttered toast & garnished
with watercress & lemon

Roasted shoulder of Lamb with
Rosemary & Almonds

New potatoes with mint
Petit pois à la française
Turnips

Rum & Apricot Gâteau
Cream

Cheese Biscuits
Crisp French Bread

Coffee

~147~

Escolop of Veal is cut from the top of the leg. The butcher will cut them for you. Then proceed as described in the recipe on page 121. Veal is sometimes difficult to buy. Pork fillet can be substituted. This is the undercut of the loin. In very young pork this is too small and cuts from the loin or the top of the leg can be used instead.

Spring is often a difficult time for vegetables ~ so many are finished and others have not begun. My ragoût de légumes is an answer. Also it is very good tempered for entertaining as once cooked it can either be re-heated or kept warm indefinitely.

Fry a chopped onion in 2oz butter. Then add every root crop you can think of cut small: carrots, parsnips, artichokes. To these add a peeled tomato, some celery and a leek. Summer all very slowly ~ no water. Finally add beurre manié to thicken the natural juice. Add salt, pepper and some chopped parsley and watercress. Usually it takes about 40 minutes.

Potatoes Anna ~ the recipe is on page 167.

Green salad can be simply lettuce, watercress tomato and cucumber. It can be made more interesting by adding chopped celery and some blanched leaves of chicory. Just have a small jug of French dressing (p 35) to toss it in at the last minute.

Ginger mousse is on page 138. The fruit salad is a safety valve as some people dislike ginger.

The cheese is not really necessary at the end but it is a nice touch. Home made cream cheese is very easy to make. Allow two pints of scaled milk to sour in an airing cupboard. The quicker it sours the sweeter the cheese will taste.

Line a big pudding basin with cheese cloth - or a clean tea-towel. Pour in the sour milk. Tie it up and let it drip into the basin. After 36 hours use the whey for the exciting soup on p.14.

Now mix the cheese well adding salt, pepper & a little fresh cream. Put it in a dish. When it has settled turn it upside down on a little piece of cloth on the drawing board. A few more hours and it is ready. It can be flavoured at the mixing time with many things: chopped chives, or walnuts & a little brandy et cetera.

## A Spring Dinner. (Menu p. 147.)

This is a particularly easy dinner to accomplish. If you don't feel like making pâté it may be bought _ or use the terrine on page 139. Toast can be made at table, or very near, with an electric toaster_ make sure that the butter is at room temperature and not hard, unco-operative and well nigh tasteless. I like to arrange the watercress as small posies in egg cups. This stops it wilting. Lemon wedges are easier to squeeze if cut as in the illustration below.

The recipe for roasted shoulder of lamb is on page 105. To give it additional flavour prick with a skewer & insert a tuft of rosemary every inch. If you have no fresh rosemary use dried & just sprinkle it over the skin. A handful of flaked almonds can be sprinkled on ½ an hour before dishing up. The recipe for sugar peas cooked with onion, lettuce & carrots is on page 58. Use this substituting frozen peas for the pois mangetout. The Turnips cooked under the shoulder recipe is on p. 105.

Gravy is something about which there is much ignorance. A good gravy can add magic to a roast. It should be a marriage of all the flavours. Pour the excess fat into a dripping pot. The joint is sitting happily on a LARGE dish _ don't forget

the carver! Now my dodge is to have the gravy
boat beside the cooker. As I cook I put in a little
of everything in the main dish: A little of the turnip
water, a little of the pea water ~ even though cooked
in butter, onion & lettuce, there is enough juice to
borrow a little ~ a little stock: When cooking this
dinner I cut off the knuckle & simmer it in the
turnip water. Now when you make the gravy
all you have to do is stir in a little plain flour
to the dish juices & brown it ~ stirring all the time
and then pour in the mixture in the gravy boat ~
bring to the boil & pour it back. This for me is
a true gravy wedded to the entire dish. You can
even add a little of the new potato water if you
like the astringent flavour of mint.
    The Rum & Apricot gateau is on p. 127.
    Cheese & biscuits need no herald. To serve
crisp french bread give it 10 minutes at No 4
in the oven.

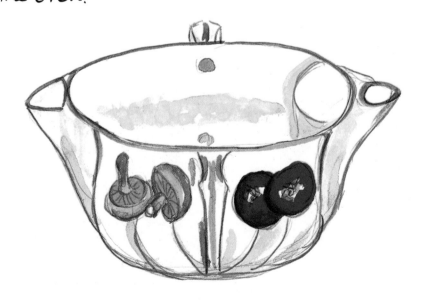

# SUMMER

The season of plenty when so many delicious things to eat appear in the garden and the shops. The first asparagus is well worth waiting for. Frozen and tinned are both enjoyable but nothing compares with the fresh vegetable, freshly cooked with melted butter. Real Scotch salmon is a treat and very expensive ~ but why pay even more for a restaurant ~ with all it's overheads ~ to cook it for you?

It is the time of ripe tomatoes, runner beans ~ the King of English vegetables. crisp lettuces. locally dug new potatoes ~ not wax bodies interred in peat from dubious foreign soil ~ strawberries, raspberries, red currants. gooseberries, blackcurrants, cherries & plums. A veritable garden of Eden time of the year. What about that truly Victorian dessert: The Summer Pudding ~ the haute cuisine of France has nothing remotely like it.

# A SUMMER LUNCHEON

Tomato Soup with
crisp French b_

Salmon Mayonnaise
Potato Salad

een Salad        Cucumber
Mayonnaise
French dressing.

Eve Pudding
Cream

Cheese
with biscuits _
Coffee

~153~

It is sad that so many really simple good things to eat are taken over by manufacturers, standardised and then hackneyed. This is the fate of tomato soup. The commercial versions are good but common or garden. A really interesting soup using fresh ripe tomatoes is on page 21. Crisp french bread p 151.

Salmon mayonnaise. Unless you can cook a whole fish it is best to use the recipe on p. 95. Mayonnaise p 26. Garnish with cucumber & lemon slices. Make a green, green salad ~ no tomatoes ~ and serve with french dressing p.35

Potato Mayonnaise is best made from cold new potatoes, mayonnaise, salt, pepper and a teaspoonful of chopped chives and one of chopped parsley.

Eve pudding is on p. 136.

This is a very simple luncheon **menu** to prepare. Although it says steam the pudding for 2 hours a longer time will not harm it.

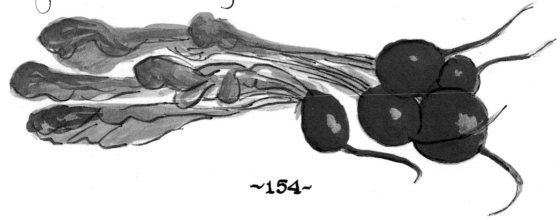

# A SUMMER DINNER

Smoked Haddock with Mushrooms
served in a Scallop shell

Filet de Boeuf Wellington
Pommes duchesse        Runner Beans
Mixed Green Salad
French dressing

Raspberry & Red Currant
Gâteau with cream

Cheese
Crisp French bread
Biscuits

Coffee

~155~

The recipe for the smoked haddock is on p.100. It is possible to prepare this hours before serving. In this event give the shells 20 minutes at No.4 and finish off under the grill.

The recipe for Boeuf Wellington is on p.103. This can be prepared in the morning or even the day before. Whatever you decide to do it needs a minimum of one hour in the fridge before baking for 35 minutes at No.7 — the lowest shelf of the oven will then be the right temperature for the scallop shells. The runner beans only need eight minutes from when they return to the boil (p56).

A mixed green salad looks pretty in the centre of the table and the French dressing will be ready in a little jug on the table. Pommes duchesse (p167) can be finished in the very top of the oven.

The gateau (p126) can be made in the morning. It is a good thing to put the raspberries on nearer the time of serving. Start in the middle & make circles round - finishing at the outer edge.
The cheese board can be left ready on the side board and the crisp french bread can take the place of the shells in the oven when these go to the grill.

This simple dinner needs a lot of forward planning but the actual party should be a great success with the hostess only missing for about 20 minutes. I usually waltz about with a glass in one hand & use the minute timer to recall me to the cooker!

# AUTUMN

The season of Game: grouse, partridge, pheasant, hare, venison and many other delights. Something that the British cook handles better than anyone. The question of hanging meat is often misunderstood. It is difficult with wild game to judge how young and tender it is. Between rigor mortis and putrefaction there is a happy medium ~ when the fibres start to break down and the meat is far more palatable. Usually a week in a cool larder is about right ~ or 10 days in the fridge ~ but the meat must hang unwrapped with a free passage of air.

With venison I make a marinade of a bottle of red wine, a bouquet garni, one onion chopped and a coffee cup of olive oil. Turn the venison each day for about five days. Pour over the marinade so that the oil settles on the top again. The marinade can be reduced to use in the gravy. Venison is best roasted very slowly ~ 4 hrs at No 1 + completely covered with the fat from a pig's belly. The dish should then be covered with silver foil else the meat becomes dry and uninteresting. In the old days the meat was larded ~ but the pig's belly fat does a good job.

# An Autumn
# LUNCHEON

Avocado Mbaraki

Pigeon Pie      Red currant jelly
Braised chicory and carrots
Baked jacket potatoes
Watercress

Pears cooked in Wine

The Cheese Board
Crisp French bread and
Biscuits.

Coffee

# An AUTUMN DINNER

Asparagus Quiche ~ served cold with pre-dinner drinks

Roasted, stuffed, shoulder of Venison
Swedes & Turnips with cream & watercress
Pommes Boulangère
French Beans
Red Currant Jelly.

Coffee Gâteau

Cheese. French Bread. Biscuits

Coffee

~159~

The avocado dish was "invented" in Kenya during the War.  For 4 portions you need 2 ripe pears.  Take a cup of real mayonnaise and thin with a very little water.  To this add one young leek, one young carrot and a handful of cashew nuts ~ all shredded or chopped.  Put this mixture into the centre of the pears. Take care to cover the surface with a little to stop this discolouring.

The recipe for the pigeon pie is on page 49.; Braised chicory and carrots on page 75.

The pears cooked in wine are a good foil to the rich pie. (P137).

The recipe for the Asparagus quiche is on p.144. Served cold, I think, it tastes better than hot. If cut into finger strips it can be served with the aperitifs and take the place of an entree.

As you only have to make gravy and cook the French beans (only 8 minutes from when they reboil) your disappearance from the party should not be for more than 10 minutes. Have a kettle on the boil for the beans and make the gravy by dishing the Venison (the marinade recipe and cooking time are on p.157) In the morning reduce the marinade and strain. This can then sit ready in the gravy boat. Make the gravy in the usual way ~ using the marinade as stock. The pan juices will be extra well flavoured because of the herb stuffing.

Get the butcher to bone the shoulder but NOT to roll it. Put it into the marinade in this state.

For the stuffing use a dessertspoonful each of chives, Parsley, Thyme, Marjoram and a sprig of rosemary. All well chopped and mixed with a cupful of fresh breadcrumbs, an egg, a lot of soft butter (about 3oz), the juice and grated rind of a lemon, salt, pepper and a touch of nutmeg.

Replace the bone cavity with the stuffing and if it looks untidy either use a couple of Skewers or darning needle and thread to sew up the wound ~ depending on whether you are a stitch in time, or a safety pin girl!

The swede and turnip recipe is on page 71. It's astringency is a good foil to the red currant jelly. This can be made ready in the morning and put at the bottom of the cool oven covered in a vegetable dish an hour before needed. The potatoes boulangère (p.167) should be at the top of the oven with the venison on the middle shelf. No 2 oven, for the top shelf will make the middle approx No 1 and the bottom even lower. Coffee gâteau is on page 126 and follows the rich venison well as it is light and not over-sweet.

Taramasalata is a Greek recipe for pâté made of smoked cod's roe. For 6 large portions use ½ lb roe, 1 slice bread (no crusts) 1 cup of olive oil, 1 egg yolk. Lemon juice salt & pepper. Wet the bread, squeeze dry. Thoroughly mix with the roe. Gradually add oil as in making mayonnaise & finally the egg yolk + then lemon juice, salt & pepper to taste. Serve with hot buttered toast & sprinkle with chives & parsley.

# WINTER

This is the time to serve the more robust dishes; casseroles made with wine, joints of meat and rich baked vegetables.

For a simple luncheon for close friends a good warming soup can be followed by cold meat, home made pickles and hot mashed potatoes followed by a good hot pudding so enjoyed by our menfolk ~ perhaps an apple one. Or this could be the time to show off with a rum soufflé omelette.

# A WINTER LUNCHEON

Oeufs Russe
served on a bed of
crisp lettuce


Belgian Casserole of Beef
Baked jacket potatoes
Braised Celery
Cole Slaw


Meringues, Palobo
and Cream


Coffee

For a more formal occasion I suggest the Winter Luncheon shown on p.163.     For the <u>Oeufs Russe</u>
1 or 1½ hard boiled eggs a portion.   Blend the yolks taken from the halved eggs with a tin of anchovy fillets ~ oil and all.   They can be piped or spooned back into the whites. Arrange on crisp lettuce.  Garnished with smoked herring fillets (p. 143) they look more important.

<u>Belgian Casserole</u> (p. 36) is a particularly interesting dish and goes well with the Cole Slaw.  There are many recipes for this  relish.   Here is the one I use:

Cole Slaw.  Use half white and half red shredded cabbage. Soak for at least an hour in French dressing. (p. 35).  It should reduce by about half as the oil attacks the fibres.  Then add some chopped chives (or a little onion forced through a garlic press.) Then it needs something crunchy ~ a little apple or celery and a shredded carrot.  Mix well and serve in an attractive dish.

<u>Braised Celery.</u>     This is a good tempered vegetable. Having washed it and cut it into suitable lengths cook gently in a very little salted water for about 10 minutes. Put it into a buttered casserole and cover with rich brown gravy.  It will sit in the oven indefinitely as long as it is closely covered.

<u>Palobo</u>  (p. 129)  and  <u>Meringues</u>  (p. 129).

Use the palobo to stick the meringues to-gether and serve with whipped cream. Chopped nuts may be mixed with the palobo.


So with everything in the oven (including the baked jacket potatoes)  and the entrée and the dessert both cold and ready ~ as well as the cole slaw ~ you can appear as the unharrassed hostess and produce this luncheon as if by magic.

# A WINTER
# DINNER

Taramasalata garnished with
parsley and chives.
Hot toast and butter.

Roasted Loin of Pork

Sage & onion stuffing          Sauce Robert

Roasted potatoes & Parsnips.
Brussels Sprouts.

Rum & Chocolate Shape.

Cheese & Crisp French Bread

Coffee

# A Winter Dinner

The Taramosalata* (p 162) is a good starter, and can be made in the morning. The Rum and chocolate shape (p 132) needs to be made early to allow time for it to set. The butter makes this more difficult but greatly adds to the quality of the end product.

Roasted Loin of Pork (p 101). With the crackling treated and really crisp, the sage and onion stuffing underneath to catch the juices and the astringent Sauce Robert (p 28) it really is a splendid dish for a cold winter night.

The potatoes and parsnips, peeled and cut in suitable sizes can be simmered together in the onion water for five minutes and then set around the joint in the oven. Turn after 40 minutes to get them evenly browned. The water goes into the gravy boat ready for making at the last minute.

Brussels sprouts (p 61) only need 8 minutes after they boil. Don't forget to use equal quantities of salt and sugar. It makes all the difference. You can dish the joint, potatoes and parsnips, and make the gravy during this 8 minutes.

As my English Granny used to say: "It's as easy as Kiss your hand!"

It is her recipe for the sage & onion stuffing. She used apple sauce the Sauce Robert comes from the Belgian Granny - Entente Cordiale.

~166~

# POTATOES ~ 3 good natured ways of serving

When cooking at home fiddling about at the last minute with potatoes can be a nuisance. Here are some easy ones:

## POTATOES ANNA.

This is particularly suitable for new potatoes. Butter an oven proof dish. Cut the potatoes into rings about ⅛" thick. Arrange them in the dish standing up on their sides until the dish is full. Add salt, pepper, several knobs of butter and a coffee cup full of milk. Give them an hour with the lid on at No 4. and then take of the lid and let them colour up. This takes about 30 minutes. They can then be left in the oven for a long while without spoiling.

## POMMES DUCHESSE
2 lbs of potatoes, peeled, cooked and mashed very thoroughly. Take 3 eggs and reserve 1 yolk. Beat the eggs and mix thoroughly with the potatoes. Taste and add salt and pepper. Butter a baking sheet and either pipe the potatoes like meringues or spoon them into little mounds. Add a little milk to the yolk + brush all over the potatoes. They can then be left in a fridge. Cook for 10 minutes in a very hot oven. (No 9).

## POMMES BOULANGERE.
Cut peeled potatoes into rings and wash in cold water. Butter a baking dish. Cut an onion small. Place potatoes in layers with salt, pepper, onion and parsley. Cover with good stock. Bake at No 2 for about 2 hours. The stock should disappear and leave the potatoes golden brown on top.

# Good-Tempered DISHES for ENTERTAINING

I call them this because they will sojourn in the oven without spoiling.

# Good-Natured Vegetables.

# OFF~WHITE BREAD

This is a really easy recipe for making crisp rolls or plaits of good bread.

1oz fresh yeast.   1 heaped teaspoon demerara sugar.
1oz dripping, butter or vegetable fat.
1 heaped teaspoon salt,   Poppy seed.
12 fluid ozs of a mixture of milk and water at blood heat.
1 handful of bran.  1 handful of wheat germ.
Approx 1½ lbs plain flour.

Put the yeast, sugar and half the fluid in a basin and beat gently.   Set aside.   Put the fat and salt into the other half of the fluid.  When the yeast starts to work (about 8 minutes) amalgamate the two liquids and beat lightly   Add two good handfuls of the flour to the mixture and stir.

Put the rest of the flour with the bran and the wheatgerm into a mixing bowl. Make a well in the centre and pour in the fluid.  Mix with a spoon.   If it is too dry add a little more tepid water.  If too sticky add a little more flour .  When you can handle it knead for about 10 minutes. Divide into 4 pieces.  Roll out with a rolling pin until about ¼" thick.  Either cut the piece into 8 squares and rub up into rolls ~ or cut into 3 and roll into sausage shapes (long).  These can be plaited and squeezed together at the ends. This quantity is enough for 16 rolls and 2 plaits. Butter a baking tin and arrange the

16 rolls on it and another for the 2 plaits. Set to prove in the fridge for about 20 minutes. Take out of the fridge and set in the Kitchen for 10 minutes while the oven is warming up at No. 7. Brush the rolls and the plaits with tepid salt water and sprinkle with poppy seed. Bake for 12 minutes then reverse the positions of the trays in the oven and bake for another 12 minutes. Take out of the oven and set upside down on wire trays to cool. Be careful. It is very easy to burn yourself. You will find that you can handle the bread but that the trays are lethal. This bread freezes beautifully.

I like to serve it hot and always give rolls or plaits made earlier in the day, or day before, 10 minutes in the oven at No 4 just before using them. The cold bread can be kept in polythene bags in the fridge for about a week or longer as long as it is refreshed in the oven this way.

# INDEX

X, y, z

The End

AW

Bonchurch
8th August 1979

# EQUIVALENT MEASURES

     I know it is now considered "with it" to think in grammes, metres and litres. ~ ~ But women of my generation know the old measures by heart and will find it hard to change. I hope these conversion tables will prove useful. They are all <u>very</u> approximate and not meant to be taken as a firm fact.

     The basis of measuring in cooking is founded on simple experience and on methods which have been proved to work.

     For instance:

To make a pint of thin sauce (ie like single cream) use 1-2 oz butter, oil or fat, 1 oz plain flour and a pint of fluid.

To make a pint of thick sauce (ie like double cream) use 2-3 oz of fat, butter or oil, 2 oz plain flour and a pint of fluid.

To make a sauce of "blancmange" like consistency use 2 oz corn flour to a pint of fluid and enrich with butter.

     My measuring CUP is a teacup ~ 6 fl. oz.
     My measuring coffee CUP is about 3 fl. oz.

    I am indebted to Peter E. Jones Esq., M.P.S., who supervised this tricky end paper. He warns us only to work in one scale at a time ~ never to mix them ~ ~